Adaptive Neuro-Fuzzy Inference System as a Universal Estimator

Edited by Constantin Voloşencu

Published in London, United Kingdom

Adaptive Neuro-Fuzzy Inference System as a Universal Estimator
http://dx.doi.org/10.5772/intechopen.111237
Edited by Constantin Voloşencu

Contributors
Abdullahi Mahmoud Aliyu, Ammar Muhammad Ibrahim, Annie Uwimana, Ardana I. Putu, Aristide Timene, Constantin Voloşencu, Ginarsa I. Made, Haman Djalo, Masud Ibrahim, Muhammad Uzair, Muljono Agung Budi, Musbahu Garba Indabawa, Nazifi Sani Shuaibu, Ndjiya Ngasop, Nrartha I. Made Ari, Rabiu Abdulkadir, Salisu Muhammad Lawan

First published in London, United Kingdom, 2024 by IntechOpen
IntechOpen is the global imprint of INTECHOPEN LIMITED, registered in England and Wales, registration number: 11086078, 167-169 Great Portland Street, London, W1W 5PF, United Kingdom

British Library Cataloguing-in-Publication Data
A catalogue record for this book is available from the British Library

Additional hard and PDF copies can be obtained from orders@intechopen.com

Adaptive Neuro-Fuzzy Inference System as a Universal Estimator
Edited by Constantin Voloşencu
p. cm.
Print ISBN 978-0-85466-152-7
Online ISBN 978-0-85466-151-0
eBook (PDF) ISBN 978-0-85466-153-4

For EU product safety concerns:
IN TECH d.o.o., Prolaz Marije Krucifikse Kozulić 3, 51000 Rijeka, Croatia,
info@intechopen.com or visit our website at intechopen.com.

Meet the editor

Prof. Dr. Constantin Voloşencu graduated as an engineer from Politehnica University Timişoara, Romania, where he also obtained a doctorate. He is currently a full professor in the Department of Automation and Applied Informatics at the same university. Prof. Voloşencu is the author of 10 books, 7 book chapters, and more than 170 papers published in journals and conference proceedings. He has also edited fourteen books and has twenty-seven patents to his name. He is a manager of research grants, editor in chief and member of international journal editorial boards, a former keynote and plenary speaker, a member of scientific committees, and chair at international conferences. Prof. Voloşencu is a science ambassador of LiveDNA and a member of the Asian Council of Science Editors (ACSE). His research areas include control systems, control of electric drives, fuzzy control systems, neural network applications, fault detection and diagnosis, sensor network applications, monitoring of distributed parameter systems, and power ultrasound applications. He has developed automation equipment for machine tools, spooling machines, high-power ultrasound processes, and more.

Contents

Preface

The processing of information using adaptive neuro-fuzzy inference systems (ANFIS) has developed significantly in the last decades, this mathematical theory being an interesting tool for researchers to solve complex scientific and technical problems. ANFIS has found applications in various sectors of human activity, such as industry, business, finance, medicine, and more. An ANFIS is built on a complex structure formed by a neural network and a Takagi–Sugeno fuzzy inference system. Since it integrates both neural networks and fuzzy logic principles, it has the potential to capture the benefits of both in a single framework. Fuzzy logic allows for a systemic mathematical treatment using acceptable human reasoning. The ANFIS thus developed can in turn deal with the uncertainties as well as learn in real applications. Hence, ANFIS is considered to be a universal estimator.

The book has five main chapters and an introductory one. The introductory chapter presents some general aspects and applications and one example of modeling multivariable nonlinear functions based on ANFIS. Chapter 2 presents a design of an ANFIS for tractor-implement tillage depth control to decrease the tractor's ploughing depth errors. Chapter 3 presents an application of solar radiation prediction using an improved ANFIS optimization ensemble. Chapter 4 presents an application of ANFIS control in power systems. The final chapter presents a perspective study on macroeconomic dynamics through the lens of the ANFIS.

The book addresses specialists who are interested in ANFIS applications and solutions in various fields. The book covers some ANFIS theoretical concepts and includes new applications of ANFIS. Published studies demonstrate the ability of ANFIS in various practical fields. Researchers in different domains developed new ANFIS concepts, applications, and tools that enhance human understanding and improve the specialist's ability to analyze, design, and implement high-performance analysis. It presents applications that focus on the methodologies used, with case studies, implementation, and testing issues.

The editor thanks the authors for their excellent contributions and understanding during the process of editing this volume. The editor wishes to thank the staff of IntechOpen who contributed to the editorial process.

Constantin Voloşencu
Department of Automation and Applied Informatics,
"Politehnica" University Timişoara,
Timişoara, Romania

Chapter 1

Introductory Chapter: ANFIS for Modeling Multivariable Nonlinear Functions

Constantin Voloşencu

1. Introduction: general aspects and applications

Treating information using fuzzy logic and neural networks has developed throughout the last decades, these mathematical theories of artificial intelligence being interesting tools for researchers to solve complex scientific and technical problems. The combination of two concepts, artificial neural networks and Takagi-Sugeno fuzzy inference, led to the development of the adaptive neuro-fuzzy inference system (ANFIS). It has learning and adaptive capabilities, to approximate nonlinear functions, and it is considered to be a universal estimator with the potential for application in nonlinear and complex systems. The purpose of the chapter is to make an introduction for this book, highlighting the diversity of possible applications of ANFIS and presenting an example of a basic application in modeling and estimation [1].

In the architecture of ANFIS, there are two parts: the premise and the consequence. The neural network architecture has five layers. The first layer is the fuzzification layer, where the membership degrees are computed. The second layer is the rule layer, that is, generating the firing strengths for the rules. The third layer normalizes the computed firing strengths. The fourth layer offers the defuzzificated values. The last layer gives the final output. Over the years, researchers have contributed to the development both on the side of artificial neural networks, with new training methods and neuron activation functions, as well as on the fuzzy logic side, with fuzzy inference, membership functions, rule bases, and tuning of parameters, resulting in complex and hybrid structures. In ANFIS approaches, various optimization methods are used such as genetic algorithms, differential evolution, particle swarm optimization, shuffled frog leaping algorithm, satin bowerbird optimization algorithms, metaheuristic techniques, or nature-inspired algorithms [2].

ANFIS, as a universal estimator, has found applications in various sectors of human activity, such as industry (mechanics, electrical engineering, power systems, electronics, and chemistry), economy, business, finance, medicine, biology, and in many scientific fields such as modeling, prediction, machine learning, big-data technologies, control systems, expert systems, and others. This concept has been used for several decades in various modeling and prediction applications. Researchers in ANFIS develop new concepts and tools which enhance human understanding and improve the specialist's ability to design and implement high-performance systems. The researches cover aspects of ANFIS architectures, optimization techniques, applications of ANFIS as a universal estimator in modeling, and prediction in different domains of activity [3–17]. Thus, several applications can be listed: in power plants and power distribution networks, in metallurgy in the design of aluminum alloys, in the chemical industry for specific wear rate modeling of poly-tetra-flouro-ethylene composites, in electrical engineering, for inductance profile estimation for switched reluctance motors, for the definition of focal length for zoom lens for digital cameras, an adaptive filtering application as channel equalizer for mobile cellular channels, in medicine, as an application in health monitoring based on multisensor, data fusion and 2D wavelet transform, in civil engineering for prediction of compressive strength of manufactured sand concrete, in tracking disasters in the environment for spatial prediction of landslide susceptibility, in computer science, for data classification, application to identifying the online bearing fault, by filtering impulse noise, or for improving estimation algorithms for distributed parameter systems using sensor networks.

2. Example

2.1 Method

ANFIS has a certain capability of modeling a nonlinear function. Because it is a neural network with five layers, it can be said that the approximation function results as a function composed of five other functions. It is possible to try to use ANFIS for modeling, approximating, or estimating a nonlinear function of several variables, but the obtained result will have a certain error greater or less depending on multiple conditions of the process of obtaining ANFIS, such as the amount of training data used, depending on the structure used for the display, depending on the training method, depending on the available computing power, and others.

ANFIS can be seen as a function of n variables, as a mathematical application on the set of real numbers with values in the set of real numbers:

$$f: R^n \rightarrow R \tag{1}$$

ANFIS is recommended among recent computing techniques because of their tools to deal with nonlinear modeling. Such an example is presented recently in [18].

We are choosing a similar example, a nonlinear function with two variables, the sinc function:

$$z = \frac{10\sin(r)}{r}, r = \sqrt{x^2 + y^2}, x \in [-10, 10], y \in [-10, 10] \tag{2}$$

The graphic of this function is presented in **Figure 1**.

The chosen example of modeling a nonlinear multivariable function is suitable to use neuro-adaptive learning.

To make calculation for this example, the neuro-fuzzy designer and fuzzy-logic designer apps from MATLAB 2018 and 2023 were used. These apps let the user to design, train, and test adaptive neuro-fuzzy inference systems, using input/output training data, as shown below.

The fuzzy inference system is a mathematical concept that has the following information flow: crisp characteristics from the inputs—membership functions—fuzzy rules for the inputs—fuzzy rules for output characteristics—output membership

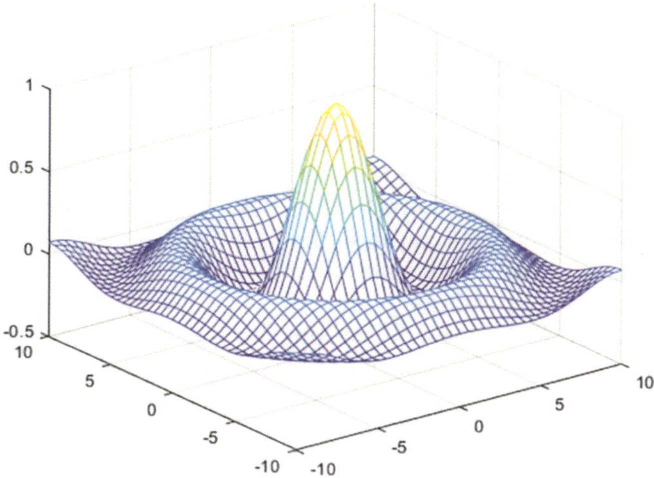

Figure 1.
Graph of the function.

functions—a single-valued output, or a decision associated with the output. So, membership functions and a rule structure are used, the processes being developed based on the user's experience of working with the process. The system applies fuzzy inference techniques. In the ANFIS concept, a neuro-adaptive learning method is used, for learning information about an input-output data set of training. The membership function parameters resulted after training. The membership functions of the fuzzy inference system are trained using a back propagation algorithm alone or in combination with a least squares method. A gradient vector is used to compute these parameters. We may say the fuzzy system can learn from the data it is modeling. The parameters of the membership functions may be changed through the learning process. The resulted neural network can interpret the input/output map. The gradient vector provides a criterion of modeling quality, in reducing the training errors. The error criterion is the sum of the squared difference between actual and desired outputs. The data are taken from Eq. (2). The modeling approach resembles system identification techniques. In the first stage, the equations are used as a parameterized model structure. This model is a relation from inputs to membership functions to rules to output to membership function and so on. In the second stage, input/output data are collected to train the ANFIS. The training data must be fully representative for the system characteristic to be modeled. A high number of samples are recommended. The second stage is the model validation, in which a set of input/output data is presented to the trained ANFIS, to see how well the ANFIS predicts the corresponding data set output values. The data set for model validation must be also representative for the system is intended to emulate, but in the same time, it must be distinct from the training data set. This is to avoid a trivial validation procedure. Again, a large amount of data is necessary. In this stage, the generalization capability of the ANFIS is checked. Also, the procedure verifies whether the model is overfitting the training data set.

The following phases are completed within the application: calculation of membership function parameters, generating an initial inference system based on the training data, establishing the structure of the system before training, avoiding overfitting using additional checking data, testing the generalization capability of the trained system using testing data, and exporting the resulted fuzzy system to the computing workspace. In this case, the fuzzy inference system is trained for one output and two inputs. A weighted average defuzzification is used. The output membership function is linear. The number of rules matches the number of output membership function. Every rule has a different consequence. It does not use custom membership functions. Neuro-fuzzy designer is an app from control system design and analysis. The neuro-fuzzy designer MATLAB application may be used for designing, training, and testing adaptive neuro-fuzzy inference systems (ANFIS), using input/output training data.

The architecture of the PC used for training consists of a processor Intel i9, 12th generation, with 3 GHz clock frequency and 32GB RAM memory at 3.4 GHz.

2.2 Results

As presented in the method, a fuzzy inference system is chosen for training, based on Sugeno-type inference, with two inputs and one output, the neural network having three hidden layers. Tests were performed with various input membership functions. The present result was obtained with generalized bell-type membership functions. Tests were performed with three and five input membership functions. The tests with five membership functions required extremely long calculation times and, contrary to expectations, gave larger mean squared errors. 16.008.001 input-output test pairs were used for training. The number of tunable parameters was 45. The optimization method was least squares estimation with backpropagation. The fuzzy inference structure was trained once from error 1.64, during 100 epochs, until error 1.032. The structure obtained after the first training was trained a second time from error 1.03 to error 0.827, during another 100 epochs. The layers of the ANFIS structure used in this example are presented in **Figure 2**. The graphs of the error variation during the two training periods are shown in **Figure 3a** and **b**. The variations of wind values, for the two workouts, are presented in **Figure 4a** and **b**. The

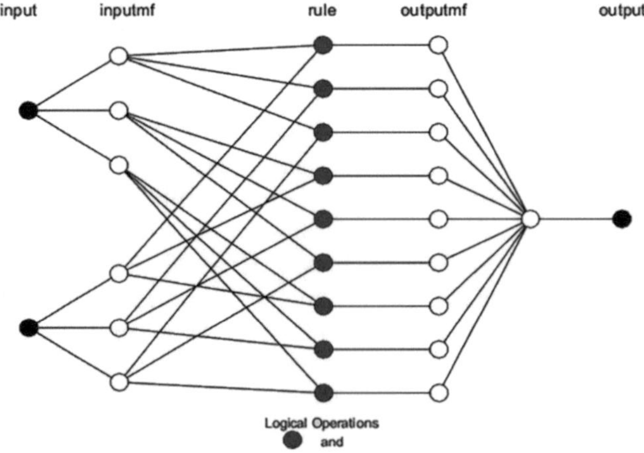

Figure 2.
ANFIS internal structure.

final, minimal training RMSE, of the ANFIS as an example, was 0.827. The structure of the tuning ANFIS is presented in **Figure 5**. The membership functions of the first input and second input are presented in **Figure 6a** and **b**. The membership functions of the output are presented in **Figure 7**. The rule base is presented in **Figure 8**. An example of ANFIS rule inference is presented in **Figure 9**. The surface of the tuned

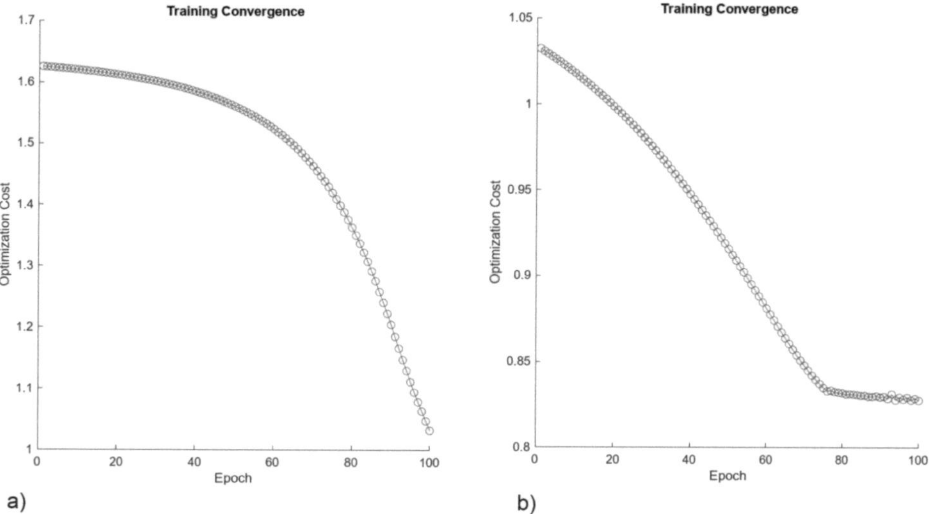

Figure 3.
Training convergence graph.

a)

```
74          1.42942
75          1.41951
76          1.4093
Step size decreases to 0.061159 after epoch 77.
77          1.39881
78          1.38804
79          1.37585
80          1.36332
Step size decreases to 0.067275 after epoch 81.
81          1.35046
82          1.33727
83          1.32241
84          1.3072
Step size decreases to 0.074002 after epoch 85.
85          1.29167
86          1.27587
87          1.25824
89          1.22252
90          1.20465
91          1.18519
92          1.16612
Step size decreases to 0.089543 after epoch 93.
93          1.14764
94          1.12994
95          1.11156
96          1.0944
Step size decreases to 0.098497 after epoch 97.
97          1.0784
98          1.06334
99          1.04753
100         1.03224

Designated epoch number reached. ANFIS training completed at epoch 100.

Minimal training RMSE = 1.03224
```

b)

```
74          0.837285
75          0.834983
76          0.833085
77          0.833405
78          0.832432
79          0.832085
80          0.831786
Step size decreases to 0.061159 after epoch 81.
81          0.8311
82          0.831221
83          0.831035
84          0.830755
85          0.830375
86          0.830422
87          0.829795
88          0.829684
89          0.83011
90          0.82942
91          0.829779
Step size increases to 0.055043 after epoch 92.
92          0.82849
93          0.831286
94          0.827667
95          0.829437
Step size increases to 0.049539 after epoch 96.
96          0.82807
97          0.829359
98          0.827593
99          0.828656
Step size increases to 0.044585 after epoch 100.
100         0.827444

Designated epoch number reached. ANFIS training completed at epoch 100.

Minimal training RMSE = 0.827444
```

Figure 4.
Numerical variation of the training error.

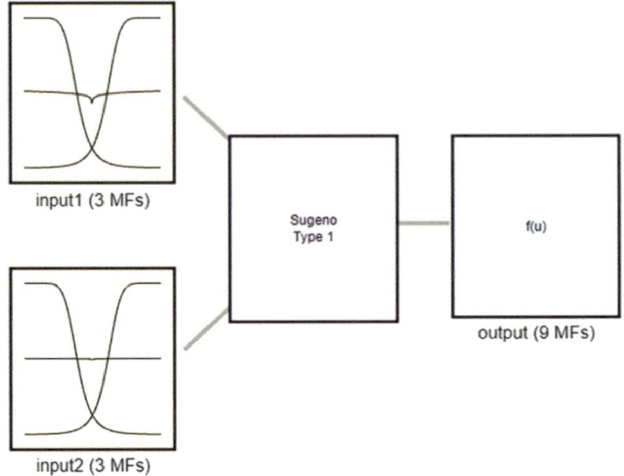

Figure 5.
ANFIS structure after training.

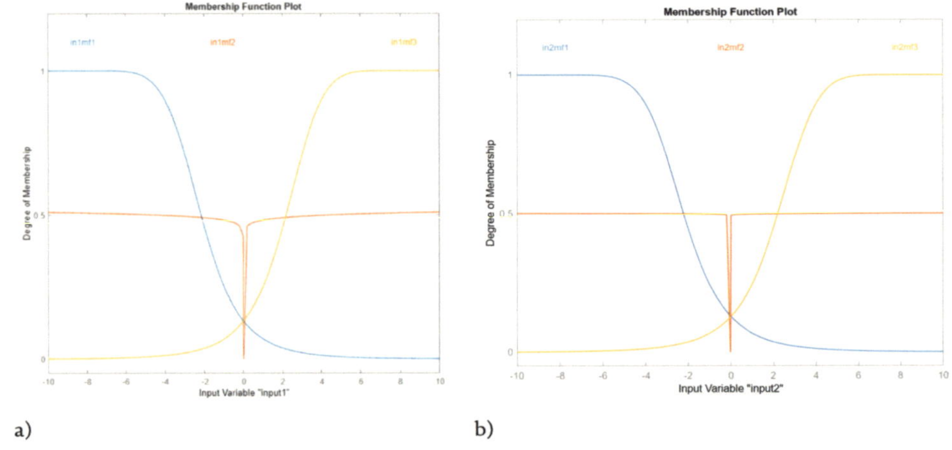

Figure 6.
(a) Membership functions of input 1. (b) Membership functions of input 2.

ANFIS is presented in **Figure 10**. **Figure 11** shows the ANFIS output after the first and second training on the same graph. The error surface obtained for the output of these two trained structures is presented in **Figure 12**. A validation set with 40.401 input-output pairs was used for validation. **Figure 13** compares the outputs of the trained ANFIS and the outputs of the training set on the same graph.

3. Conclusion

The chapter presents an example of the development of an ANFIS structure for modeling the function sinc, a nonlinear function of two variables. The stages through which training and validation were carried out are presented. Training results are presented. The ANFIS structure is a standard one, with two inputs, three membership

Name	Type	Parameters
out1mf1	Linear	[1.3644 1.52369 40.397]
out1mf2	Linear	[-2.38457 -0.0363462 -56....
out1mf3	Linear	[1.36348 -1.48706 40.3859]
out1mf4	Linear	[0.0250792 -2.67636 -57.4...
out1mf5	Linear	[-0.0573503 0.0716386 74...
out1mf6	Linear	[0.0251667 2.60579 -57.4...
out1mf7	Linear	[-1.39102 1.52443 40.4119]
out1mf8	Linear	[2.43925 -0.0363729 -55.9...
out1mf9	Linear	[-1.39006 -1.4878 40.4006]

Figure 7.
The membership functions of the output.

	Rule	Weight	Name
1	If input1 is in1mf1 and input2 is in2mf1 then output is out1mf1	1	rule1
2	If input1 is in1mf1 and input2 is in2mf2 then output is out1mf2	1	rule2
3	If input1 is in1mf1 and input2 is in2mf3 then output is out1mf3	1	rule3
4	If input1 is in1mf2 and input2 is in2mf1 then output is out1mf4	1	rule4
5	If input1 is in1mf2 and input2 is in2mf2 then output is out1mf5	1	rule5
6	If input1 is in1mf2 and input2 is in2mf3 then output is out1mf6	1	rule6
7	If input1 is in1mf3 and input2 is in2mf1 then output is out1mf7	1	rule7
8	If input1 is in1mf3 and input2 is in2mf2 then output is out1mf8	1	rule8
9	If input1 is in1mf3 and input2 is in2mf3 then output is out1mf9	1	rule9

Figure 8.
The rules of inference.

functions for each input, an inference layer with nine nodes and one output with linear activation function. This structure was trained using a huge amount of training pair data. Many training sessions were made, with different parameters. The training was made in two stages, both with 100 epochs, to reduce the training error. The error decreased aperiodic, asymptotically. The descending step of backpropagation was modified automatically at several epochs. The training had to adapt 45 parameters, including the membership functions of the input and output. The membership functions had the shape of the generalized bell. The membership functions of the two inputs are similar. The membership functions of the output, in the number of nine, are linear. The rule base has nine rules. The example shows that a large number of trainings are necessary, using various ANFIS structures and various training sets, and also as a result of the experiments carried out, it turned out that huge computing resources are needed, with millions of training sets and high computing power. The duration of the calculations for training amounted to several hours. After the tests, a structure may be chosen that resulted with a minimum mean squared error.

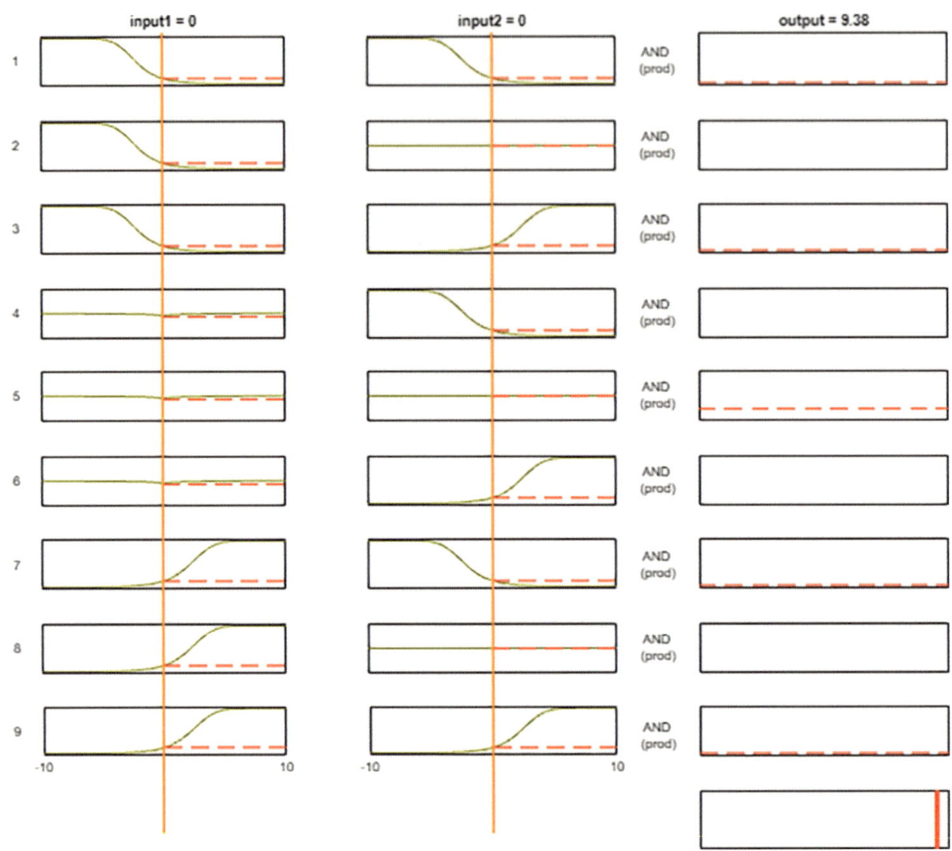

Figure 9.
Example of an inference graph.

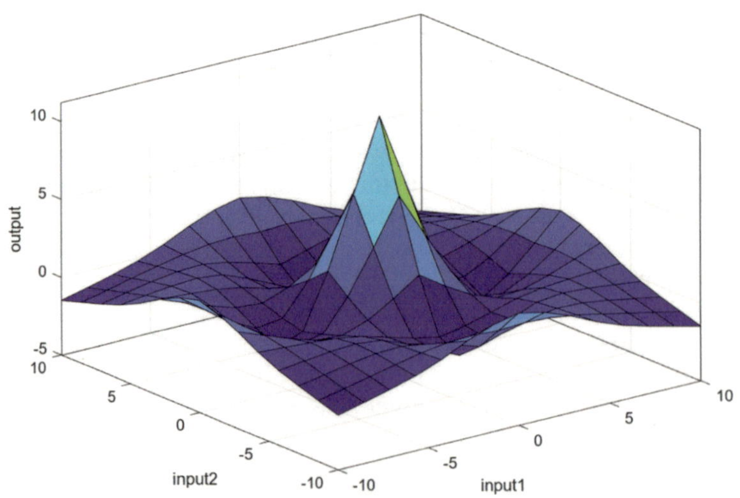

Figure 10.
Graph of the ANFIS function.

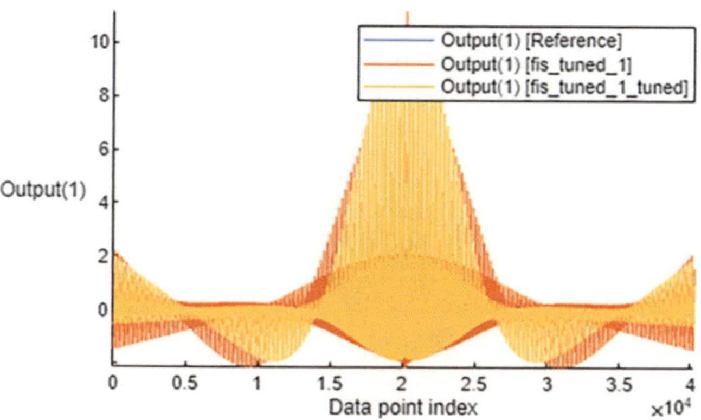

Figure 11.
Output graphs after the first and second training.

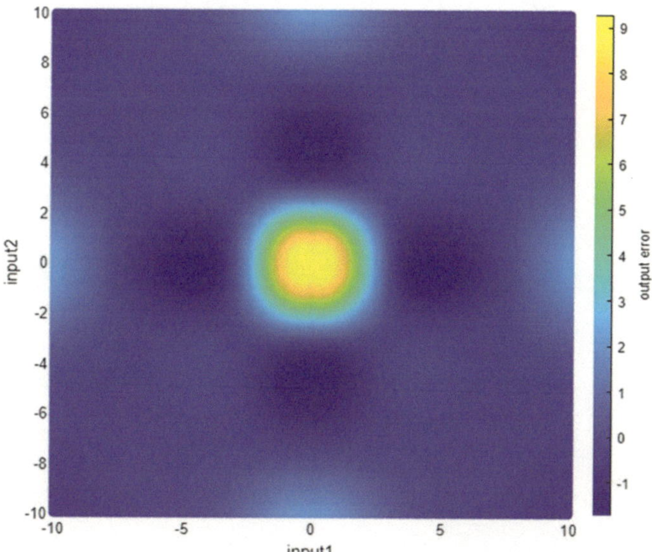

Figure 12.
Spatial plot of errors.

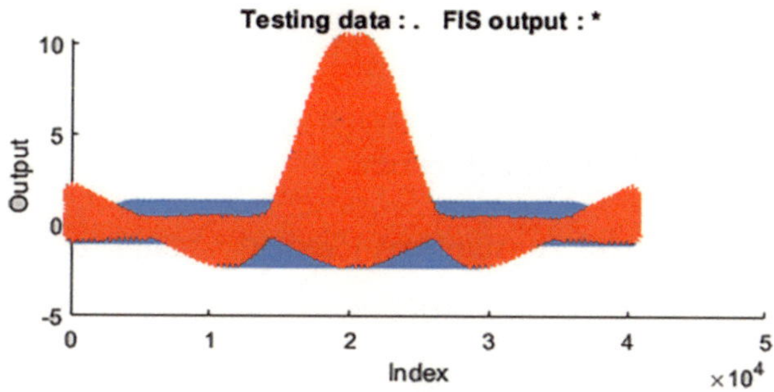

Figure 13.
Output graphs: blue – for training data, red – validation output.

The approximation errors vary a lot on the surface of the nonlinear function, being on certain portions small, acceptable, but on other portions quite large, having to be reduced through other attempts. It is likely that, by doing other trainings, a structure can be obtained that ensures, maybe, smaller approximation errors, but there is no such sure certainty.

Author details

Constantin Voloşencu
"Politehnica" University, Timisoara, Romania

*Address all correspondence to: constantin.volosencu@aut.upt.ro

References

[1] Jang JSR, Sun CT. Neuro-Fuzzy and Soft Computing: A Computational Approach to Learning and Machine Intelligence. Upper Saddle River, NJ: Prentice Hall; 1997. 614 p

[2] Chopra S, Dhiman G, Sharma A, Shabaz M, Shukla P, Arora M. Taxonomy of adaptive neuro-fuzzy inference system in modern engineering sciences. Computational Intelligence and Neuroscience. 2021;**14**:6455592. DOI: 10.1155/2021/6455592

[3] Aceves-Fernandez MA, editor. Artificial Intelligence—Emerging Trends and Applications. London: InTech; 2018. DOI: 10.5772/intechopen.75575

[4] Dadios E, editor. Advances in Fuzzy Logic Systems. London: IntechOpen; 2023. DOI: 10.5772/intechopen.103986

[5] Ramakrishnan S, editor. Modern Fuzzy Control Systems and its Applications. London: InTech; 2017. DOI: 10.5772/65834

[6] Suzuki K, editor. Artificial Neural Networks—Architectures and Applications. London: InTech; 2013. DOI: 10.57772/3409

[7] Volosencu C, editor. Fuzzy Logic. London: IntechOpen; 2020. DOI: 10.5772/intechopen.77460

[8] Jaude AA, editor. Forecasting in Mathematics—Recent Advances, New Perspectives and Applications. London: IntechOpen; 2021. DOI: 10.5772/intechopen.93422

[9] Garcia L, editor. Adaptive Filtering Applications. London: InTech; 2011. DOI: 10.5772/16266

[10] Savkovic B, Kovac P, Dudic B, Rodic D, Taric M, Gregus M. Application of an adaptive neuro-fuzzy inference system in Modeling cutting temperature during hard turning. Applied Sciences. 2019;**9**:3739. DOI: 10.3390/app9183739

[11] Abuhasel KA. A comparative study of regression model and the adaptive neuro-fuzzy conjecture systems for predicting energy consumption for jaw crusher. Applied Sciences. 2019;**9**:3916. DOI: 10.3390/app9183916

[12] Ly HB, Pham BT, Dao DV, Le VM, Le LM, Le TT. Improvement of ANFIS model for prediction of compressive strength of manufactured sand concrete. Applied Sciences. 2019;**9**:3841. DOI: 10.3390/app9183841

[13] Chen W, Hong H, Panahi M, Shahabi H, Wang Y, Shirzadi A, et al. Spatial prediction of landslide susceptibility using GIS-based data mining techniques of ANFIS with whale optimization algorithm and Grey wolf optimizer. Applied Sciences. 2019;**9**:3755. DOI: 10.3390/app9183755

[14] Volosencu C. Identification in sensor networks. In: Automation & Information: Theory and Advanced Technology, Proceedings of the 9th WSEAS International Conference on Automation and Information (ICAI'08); 24-26 June 2008; Bucharest, Romania. WSEAS; 2008. pp. 175-183

[15] Volosencu C. Stabilization of fuzzy control systems. WSEAS Transactions on Systems and Control. 2008;**10**:879-896

[16] Volosencu C, Curiac DI. Efficiency improvement in multi-sensor wireless network based estimation algorithms for distributed parameter systems with

application at the heat transfer. EURASIP Journal on Advances in Signal Processing. 2013;**4**. DOI: 10.1186/1687-6180-2013-4

[17] Volosencu C, Curiac DI. Monitoring distributed parameter systems based on a sensor network and ANFIS. In: Proceedings of the 2010 IEEE World Congress on Computational Intelligence IJCN; 18-23 July 2010; Barcelona, Spain. pp. 2272-2279

[18] Olatunji MO, Horsfall IT, Ukoha-Onuoha E, Osa-aria K. Application of hybrid ANFIS-based non-linear regression modeling to predict the oil yield from grape peels: Effect of process parameters and FIS generation techniques. Cleaner Engineering and Technology. 2022;**6**:100371. DOI: 10.1016/j.clet.2021.100371

Chapter 2

Design of an Adaptive Neuro-Fuzzy Inference System (ANFIS) for Tractor-Implement Tillage Depth Control

Aristide Timene, Ndjiya Ngasop and Haman Djalo

Abstract

During ploughing operations, variations in soil conditions cause ploughing depth errors. This chapter presents the designed of a neuro-fuzzy controller to decrease tractors ploughing depth errors. The tractor's electrohydraulic lifting system consisting of pump, valves and cylinders, position and force sensors, and the neuro-fuzzy controller, is modeled using MATLAB software. The aim of this study is to control the draft force and the position of the lifting mechanism using a controller based on the Adaptive Neuro-fuzzy Inference System (ANFIS). After several simulations, the performance of the proposed controller is analysed and compared with that of a Proportional Integral Derivative (PID) controller and a fuzzy logic controller. The performance index based on the Integral Time Absolute value Error (ITAE) criterion indicates a value of 0.32 in the case of the neuro-fuzzy controller; this is almost half the value of the PID controller, which is 0.76. In addition, the values of the standard deviations on the desired depth for the proposed controller are lower than those obtained by the PID controller and those of the fuzzy controller. The results obtained show that the neuro-fuzzy controller adapts perfectly to the dynamics of the system with rejection of disturbances.

Keywords: neuro-fuzzy controller, ploughing depth, tractor-implement, hitch mechanism, electro-hydraulic system, simulation

1. Introduction

From the very beginning of our existence, human beings have worked the land and produced their own food to sustain life. Good soil preparation helps crops get off to a good start, improves water infiltration and facilitates root penetration. There is generally a correlation between ploughing depth and crop yield gain. Tractors are the main source of power for ploughing implements. For optimum tractor performance during soil preparation, the tractor's electro-hydraulic lifting system is used to control

 IntechOpen

ploughing depth [1]. The tractor's electro-hydraulic lifting system consists of three main parts, namely the three-point hitch mechanism, a hitch control valve, and an electronic control unit. The tractor's three-point hitch mechanism was invented by Harry Fergusson in 1925 to lift, lower and transport hitched implements. When ploughing, the system remains in a floating position so that the plough operates at a constant working depth and can follow the soil surface even in undulating conditions [2].

On an agricultural tractor, the following operating modes are possible, position control and draft control [1]. Draft control adjusts the depth of the implement under the soil according to the force value from the ground during the tillage process. The force applied from equipment to the tractor depends on the equipment depth, soil characteristics, and vehicle velocity. In the position control, the control system arranges the height of the mechanism according to the given angle input. To improve the control accuracy of a tractor's electro-hydraulic lifting systems, P. Suomi et al. [2] designed a Proportional Integral Derivative (PID) controller to adjust the seeding depth of a tractor mounted seed drill. However, variations in soil structure were the main cause of system disturbances and errors during seeding. Moreover, the tractor's electro-hydraulic system is strongly non-linear and time-lag and the PID controller which is linear control, cannot solve the problems. Han et al. [3] designed a fuzzy logic controller to adjust the tillage depth of the implement. This controller made it possible to decrement variations in ploughing depth while increasing the tractor's tractive efficiency. Subsequently, Shafaei et al. [4] developed a fuzzy controller for ploughing depth as a function of draft force for various agricultural implements. The results indicated that the application of fuzzy controller rather than the standard controller available on the tractor resulted in an increase in tractive efficiency and overall energy efficiency. In addition, ploughing depth error, drive wheel slip and fuel consumption were reduced.

Although the fuzzy controller achieve good control accuracy, there are still some short-comings to overcome, including the designing of fuzzy inference system. The design of fuzzy inference system is based on knowledge acquired by expert operators. However, operators may not be able to translate their knowledge and experience into the form of a fuzzy logic controller. In addition, sometimes the area of expertise is not available. So it would be interesting to have algorithms for automatically learning fuzzy parameters (sets and fuzzy rules). One method for meeting these requirements is the Adaptive Neuro-fuzzy Inference System (ANFIS). This study uses the simulation software to design a neuro-fuzzy controller for tractor's electro-hydraulic lifting system based on ANFIS.

Indeed, Adaptive Neuro-Fuzzy Inference System (ANFIS) have been widely employed in control engineering with satisfactory in terms of high robustness, easy settling time, zero peaks overflow [5–8]. The remainder of the chapter is organised as follows. The second section presents the hitch-implement model. The third section describes the electro-hydraulic actuator model. The fourth section presents the control strategy. The fifth section present the MATLAB/Simulink simulation and the obtained results are commented. The last section conclude the chapter.

2. Modelling of hitch-implement mechanism

2.1 Kinematic and dynamic analysis

Modelling begins with a kinematic and dynamic analysis of the hitch-implement system. In the study proposed by Bentaher et al. [9], the coordinates of each joint are calculated in the Cartesian reference frame (x_o, y_o, z_o) with I_o, the center of the shaft connecting the rear wheels, as the point of origin. G is the tillage application point. **Figure 1** shows the different views of the system to be modelled. In this figure, the lower links are identified by B_1D_1 and B_2D_2 of identical length L_1, the lift rods are identified by A_1C_1 and A_2C_2 of identical length L_2, the lift arms are identified by O_1A_1 and O_2B_2 of identical length L_3, and the upper link is identified by EK of length L_4, rock shaft angular position. The longitudinal component of the (tillage force) draft load is F_x, the vertical component of the draft load is F_y, and the lateral component is F_z.

To simplify the calculation of forces, the three-point hitch system is modelled by ties and pin joints. The position of the implement on the ground is determined by the following equations:

$$x_G = x_D + IH\left(\frac{y_K - y_D}{IK}\right) + HG\left(\frac{x_K - x_D}{IK}\right) \tag{1}$$

$$y_G = y_D - HG\left(\frac{y_K - y_D}{IK}\right) + IH\left(\frac{x_D - x_K}{IK}\right) \tag{2}$$

A calculation program is then developed to determine these coordinates. The inputs to this program are the characteristics of the tractor taking into account the Cartesian coordinates of O, B, E, and the parameters L_1, L_2, L_3, L_4, IK, IH, HG.

Figure 2 shows the forces acting on the system, Cg and mg are respectively the centre of gravity and the weight of the implement frame, and Ri is the reaction at point i.

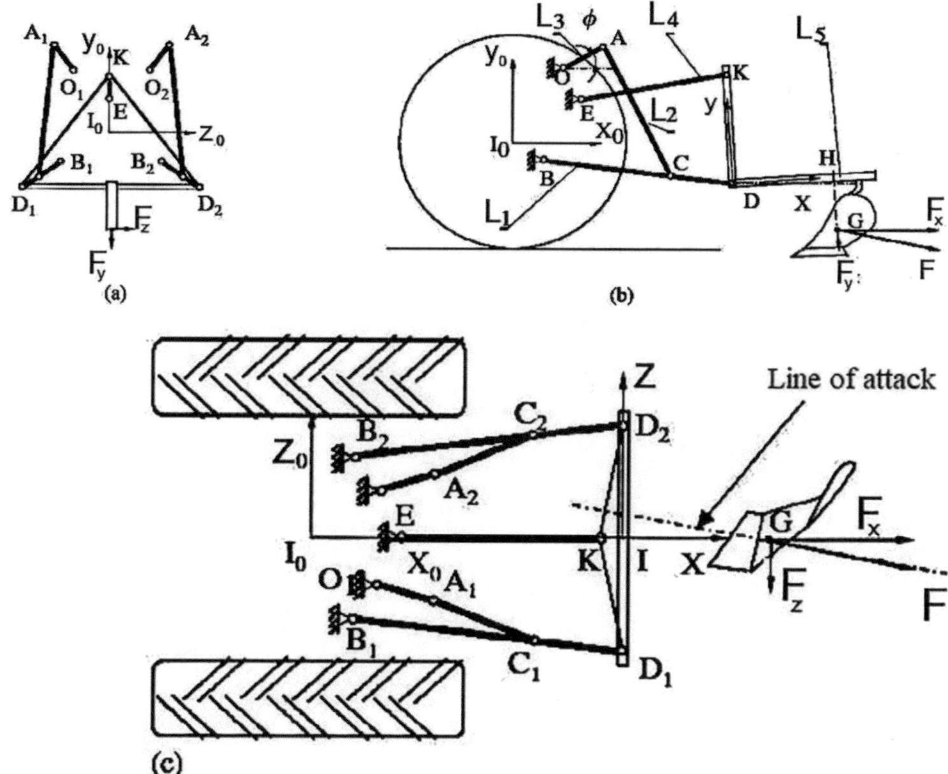

Figure 1.
Rear view (a), side view (b) and upper view (c) of the hitch-implement system.

The equilibrium of the lower left link is determined by the system of equations below:

$$
\begin{gathered}
{}^{g}R_{Dx} + {}^{g}R_{Bx} + {}^{g}R_{Cx} = 0 \\
{}^{g}R_{Cy}(z_C - z_B) - {}^{g}R_{Cz}(y_C - y_B) + {}^{g}R_{Dy}(z_D - z_B) - {}^{g}R_{Dz}(y_D - y_B) = 0 \\
{}^{g}R_{Cx}(y_C - y_B) - {}^{g}R_{Cy}(x_C - x_B) + {}^{g}R_{Dx}(y_D - y_B) - {}^{g}R_{Dy}(x_D - x_B) = 0 \\
{}^{g}R_{Cy}(x_C - x_B) - {}^{g}R_{Cx}(z_C - z_B) + {}^{g}R_{Dz}(x_D - x_B) - {}^{g}R_{Dx}(z_D - z_B) = 0 \\
\frac{{}^{g}R_{Cx}}{(x_A - x_C)} = \frac{{}^{g}R_{Cy}}{(y_A - y_C)} = \frac{{}^{g}R_{Cz}}{(z_A - z_C)} = \frac{{}^{g}R_C}{L_2}
\end{gathered}
\tag{3}
$$

here, Rij is the reaction at point "i" along the direction "j", x_i, y_i and z_i are the Cartesian coordinates of point "i" and "g" indicates the left side of the hitch-implement system [9]. The balance of the lower right-hand link is similar (with d for the right-hand side). The system of equations below is derived from the equilibrium position of the implement (**Figure 2**):

$$
\begin{cases}
F_x = {}^{g}R_{Dx} + {}^{d}R_{Dx} + R_K\left(\dfrac{x_K - x_E}{L_4}\right) \\
F_z = {}^{g}R_{Dz} + {}^{d}R_{Dz} \\
F_y = {}^{g}R_{Dy} + {}^{d}R_{Dy} + R_K\left(\dfrac{y_K - y_E}{L_4}\right) + mg \\
z_D\left({}^{d}R_{Dy} - {}^{g}R_{Dy}\right) = F_z(y_G - y_D) + mg(z_{Cg}) \\
\left[(y_K - y_D)(x_K - x_E) - (x_K - x_D)(y_K - y_E)\right]\dfrac{R_K}{L_4} = F_x(y_G - y_D) - F_x(x_G - x_D) + mg(x_{Cg} - x_I) \\
F_z = \dfrac{\left({}^{d}R_{Dx} - {}^{g}R_{Dx}\right)}{(x_G - x_D)} z_D
\end{cases}
\tag{4}
$$

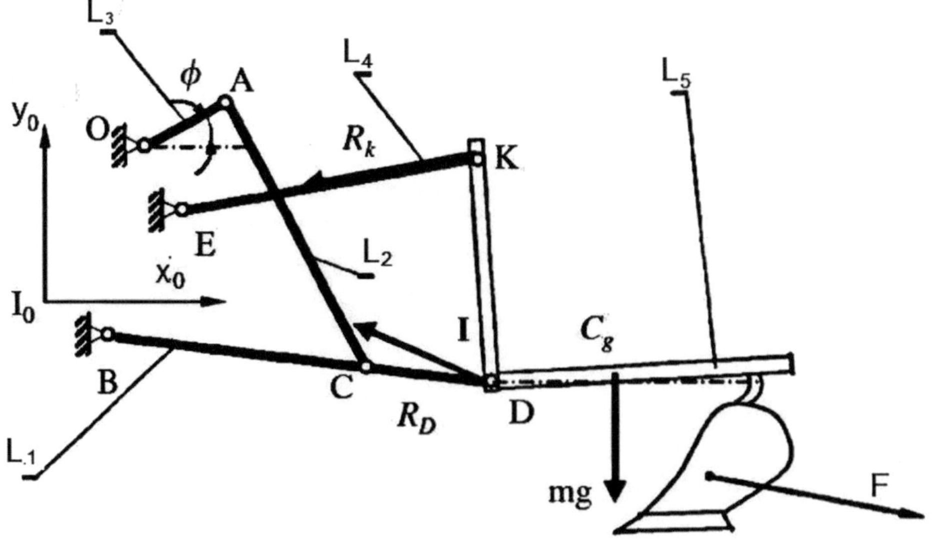

Figure 2.
Force diagram of the hitch-implement system.

Here, F_x, F_y and F_z are the orthogonal components of the draft load at point G. The solutions of these equations give the three orthogonal components of the draft load.

$$F_x = \left[\frac{(x_K - x_E)(x_D - x_B)(y_K - y_D) + (x_G - x_K)(x_D - x_B)(y_K - y_E) - (x_K - x_E)(x_G - x_D)(y_D - y_B)}{(x_D - x_B)(y_G - y_D) - (x_G - x_D)(y_D - y_B)}\right] \times \frac{R_K}{L_4} + \left[\frac{(x_C - x_B)(y_A - y_C) - (x_A - x_C)(y_C - y_B)}{(x_D - x_B)(y_G - y_D) - (x_G - x_D)(y_D - y_B)}\right]\frac{(x_D - x_G)}{L_2}\left[{}^{g}R_C + {}^{d}R_C\right] + \frac{(x_D - x_B)(x_G - x_{Cg})}{(x_D - x_B)(y_G - y_D) - (x_G - x_D)(y_D - y_B)} mg \tag{5}$$

$$F_z = \left[\frac{(x_C - x_B)(y_A - y_C) - (x_A - x_C)(y_C - y_B)}{(x_D - x_B)(y_G - y_D) - (x_G - x_D)(y_D - y_B)}\right]\frac{z_D}{L_2}\left[{}^{g}R_C + {}^{d}R_C\right] + \frac{(x_B - x_D)z_{Cg}}{(x_D - x_B)(y_G - y_D) - (x_G - x_D)(y_D - y_B)} mg \tag{6}$$

$$F_y = \left[\frac{(x_K - x_E)(y_K - y_G)(y_D - y_B) + (x_D - x_K)(y_K - y_E)(y_D - y_B) + (x_D - x_B)(y_K - y_E)(y_G - y_D)}{(x_D - x_B)(y_G - y_D) - (x_G - x_D)(y_D - y_B)}\right] \times \frac{R_K}{L_4} + \left[\frac{(x_C - x_B)(y_A - y_C) - (x_A - x_C)(y_C - y_B)}{(x_D - x_B)(y_G - y_D) - (x_G - x_D)(y_D - y_B)}\right]\frac{(y_D - y_G)}{L_2}\left[{}^{g}R_C + {}^{d}R_C\right] + \frac{(x_D - x_B)(y_G - y_D) - (x_{Cg} - x_D)(y_D - y_B)}{(x_D - x_B)(y_G - y_D) - (x_G - x_D)(y_D - y_B)} mg \tag{7}$$

These equations allow the hitch-implement mechanism to be sized according to the category of tractor. As there is a wide variety of implements, the three-point linkage must be designed taking into account the standards for agricultural machinery, in order to connect each implement smoothly to the tractor [10, 11]. Tractors are divided into four main categories (**Table 1**), and the design constraints for the three-point hitch mechanism are established according to the tractor category.

2.2 Computer-aided design

The tractor three-point hitch mechanism was modelled in SolidWorks. The mechanical assembly of the system is shown in **Figure 3**. The tractor used is a Category 2, with a maximum lifting capacity of 3546 kg and 90 horsepower [10, 12].

The base of the cylinder is fixed to the main frame of the tractor, its rod to the lifting arm, and it has a total stroke of 180 mm. In the remainder of this work, we use data supplied by the Nebraska Tractor Test Laboratory to design the three-point hitch

Category	Engine Power (kw)
1	Up to 48
2	Up to 92
3	80 to 185
4	150 to 350

Table 1.
Tractor categories [10].

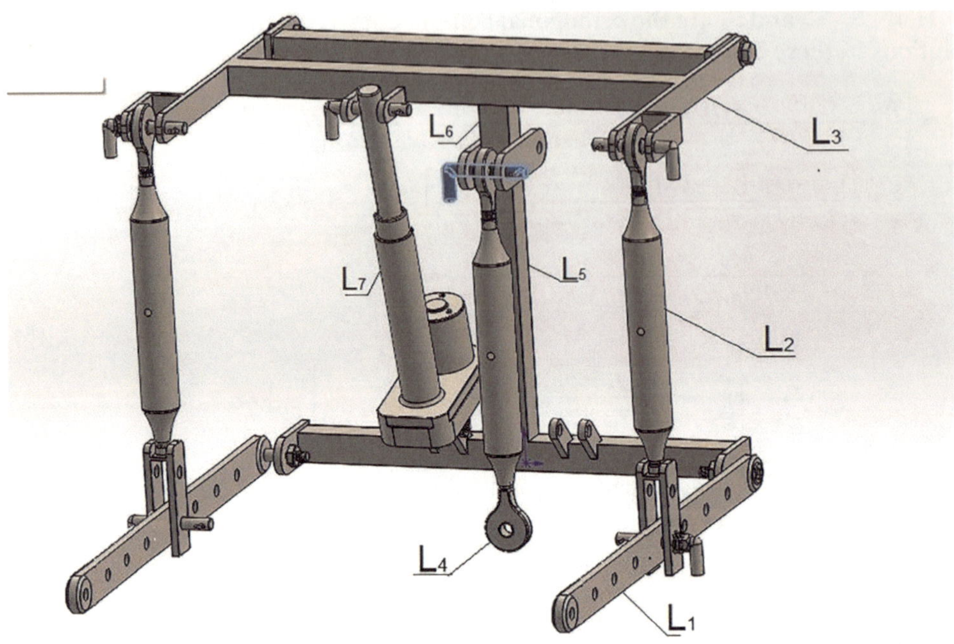

Figure 3.
Computer aided design (CAD) of a tractor three-point hitch mechanism.

mechanism [12]. The dimensions of the model are given in **Table 2**. **Figure 4** shows different views of the modelled three-point hitch mechanism.

The necessary connections such as cylindrical, revolute and spherical joints are defined in SolidWorks. The CAD model is then exported to MATLAB/Simscape Multibody. This is an XML data file of the Solidworks model. This is done using the "smimport" function. The data in this file contains the block parameters for MATLAB/Simscape Multibody. Since the entire mechanism is exported from

Part name	Measure
Lower link length (L_1)	946 mm
Lift rod length (L_2)	765 mm
Lift arm length (L_3)	295 mm
Upper link length (L_4)	650 mm
Vertical length from upper link pivot point to lower link pivot point (L_5)	460 mm
Vertical length from lift arm pivot point to upper link pivot point (L_6)	130 mm
External lift cylinder length (L_7)	380–560 mm
Stroke of the cylinder	180 mm
Mast Height	610 mm

Table 2.
Three-point linkage parameters [12].

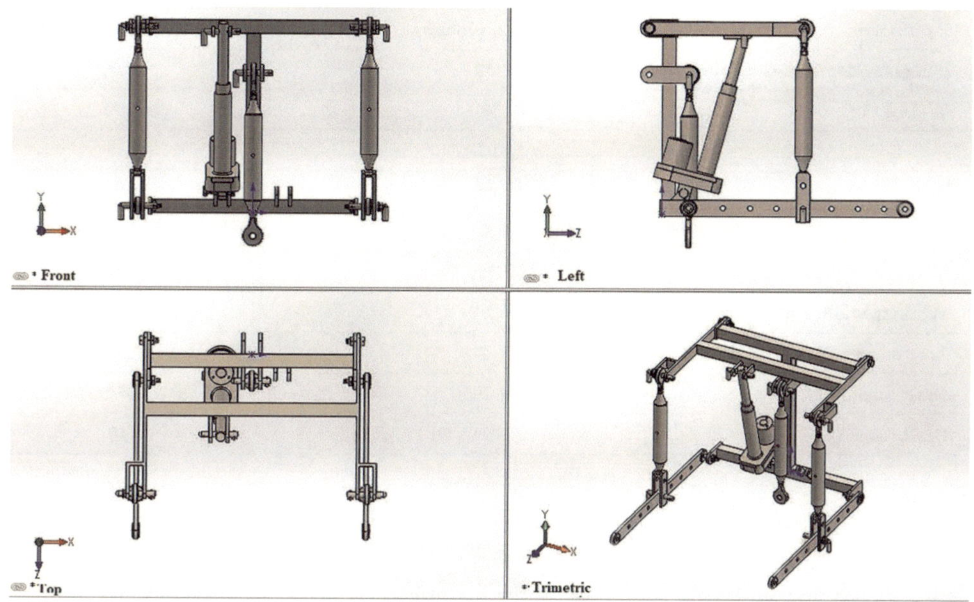

Figure 4.
Front view, left view, top view and trimetric view of the three-point hitch mechanism in SolidWorks.

SolidWorks, all moments of inertia and masses are taken into account. Once in MATLAB, the implement properties are defined. The MATLAB model of the hitch-implement mechanism is shown in **Figure 5**.

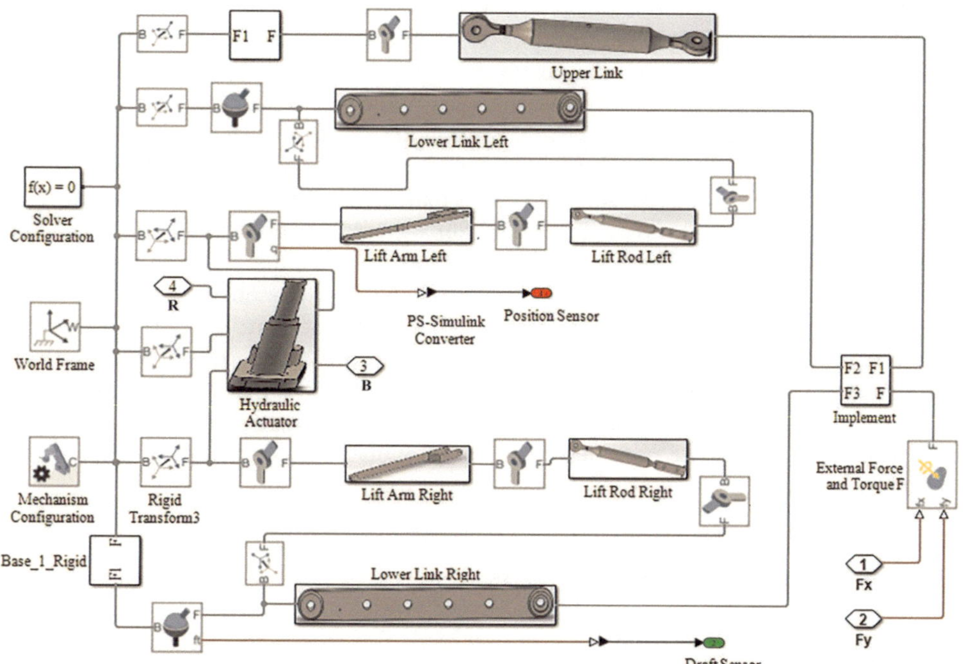

Figure 5.
Hitch-implement mechanism in MATLAB.

Parameters	Chisel plough	Moldboard plough
ploughing depth(cm)	30	10
Weight (kg)	380	200
A	107	116
B	6.3	0
C	0	2.3
Soil type	clay	Fine
Working width (m)	2.1	1.04
Tractor speed(km/h)	7	5
Draft force (N)	8095	2429
Draft range (%)	50	40

Table 3.
Implement and field parameters [13].

In this work, two implements were used: a chisel plough and a moldboard plough. The parameters of the implement and the soil resistance (draft load) corresponding to each type of soil are provided by ASABE (American Society of Agricultural and Biological Engineers) [13]. The draft load is expressed by:

$$F = T_s \times \left[a + b \times V + c \times V^2\right] \times W_e \times H_d \tag{8}$$

with, F the implement draft load (N), T_s the soil texture for a category s. a, b and c are parameters of the second order polynomial fit. a is in N/cm per unit, b is in N/cm per unit per m/s, c is in N/cm per unit per m^2/s^2. V is the tractor speed (m/s). We is the width of the implement (m) or the number of tines. H_d is the ploughing depth (cm).

The Simulink model of the hitch-implement mechanism has four inputs as shown in **Figure 5**. Ports B and R are the inlets through which the oil supplied by the hydraulic valve drives the cylinder. The other two inputs are the components of the draft load (F_x and F_y), its represent the disturbances due to the structure of the ground, acting on the implement (**Table 3**). As lateral forces are neglected, the z axis is not taken into account. The Simulink model has two outputs. The red block represents the signal from the lifting arm and the green block represents the signal from the lower links. The resistance of the soil imposes a significant draft load on the tractor. This draft force is measured using sensors located on the lower links. The position of the implement is measured using sensors located on the lifting arms. The hitch-implement mechanism is controlled by interpreting the values measured by these sensors. **Table 3** shows the parameters of the implement used; details of the variables can be found in [13].

3. Modelling the electro-hydraulic system

The actuator of the hitch-implement mechanism is the tractor's electrohydraulic system (**Figure 6**). It comprises three main parts: a hydraulic pump, a servo-valve and a cylinder. Two signals act on the valve coils to open and close the servo-valve ports. Ports B and R are the outputs from the actuator to the hitch-implement mechanism.

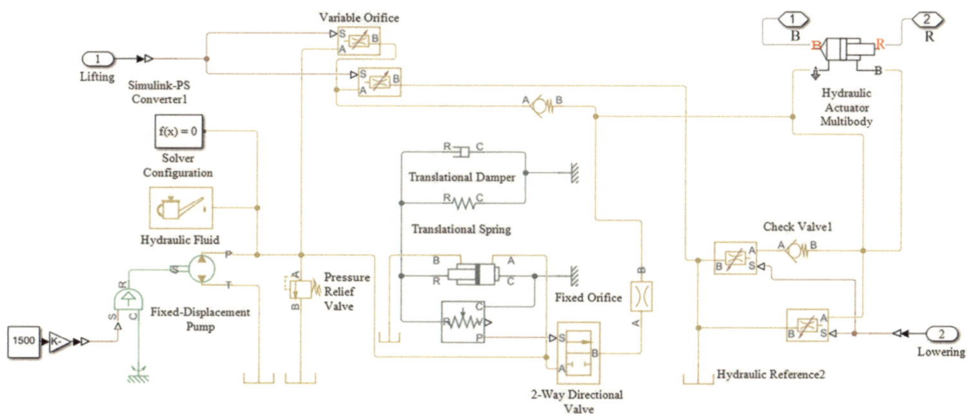

Figure 6.
Tractor's electrohydraulic hitch system.

3.1 Pump modelling

The tractor engine drive the pump at 1500 rpm. It supplies a flow rate of 60 l/min. The pressure is limited to 194 bar with a pressure limiter fitted to the main distribution block limits. **Table 4** gives the parameters of the pump used.

The flow rate of the hydraulic circuit (Q) is expressed as follows:

$$Q(\mathrm{l/\,min}) = C_{yl}\,\left(\mathrm{cm}^3/\mathrm{tr}\right) \times \omega\,(\mathrm{rpm})/1000 \tag{9}$$

Oil is one of the most critical parameters in a hydraulic system. Depending on the specification of the oil, the characteristics of the system could be radically altered. Most tractor manufacturers recommend Opet Fulltrac Fluid X 10 W-30 hydraulic oil [14]. Since the specifications of SAE30 oil are very similar to those of Opet Fulltrac Fluid X 10 W-30 oil, SAE30 oil is chosen as the system oil in Simulink.

Once the hydraulic flow has been pressurised using the pump, it is routed to the servo-valve along a line. To control the hydraulic flow, a servo-valve is used in the system. On the tractor, the servo-valve controls are electrics.

3.2 Modelling the lift valve

The BOSCH EHR5 type, two-module servo-valve is used to direct the flow of oil from the pump to the cylinder [15]. **Figure 7** shows the hydraulic circuit of the valve. The pressure compensator (1), the lifting module (2), the lowering module (3) and the non-return valve (4) are the valve components. With **A** the oil line from the valve

Description	Symbol	Value	Unit
Pump displacement	C_{yl}	25,4	$\mathrm{cm}^3/\mathrm{tr}$
Maximum system pressure	p_m	194	bar
Maximum engine speed	ω_m	2300	tr/min
Pump/motor ratio	K	1,08	

Table 4.
Hydraulic pump parameters.

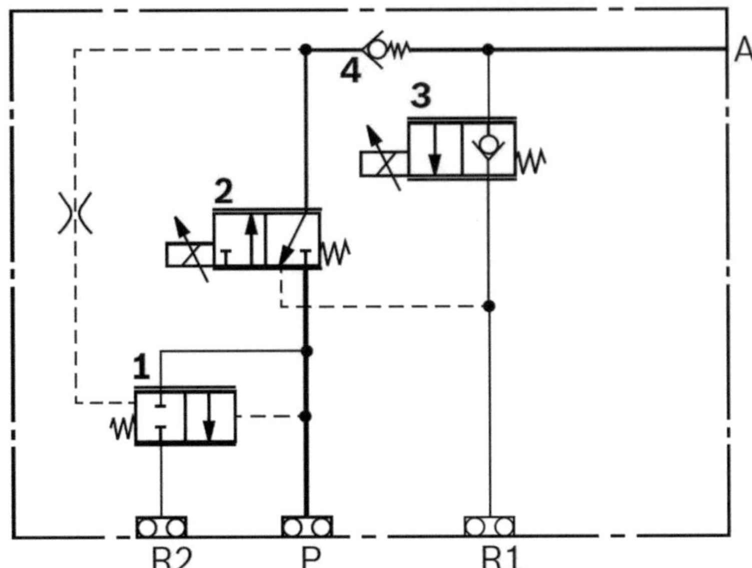

Figure 7.
Hydraulic circuit of the BOSCH EHR5 valve [15].

to the cylinder, **P** the line from the pump to the valve, $\mathbf{R_1}$ the line allowing the return of oil from the cylinder to the tank, $\mathbf{R_2}$ the line allowing the return of valve oil from the compensator to the tank.

3.2.1 Modelling the pressure compensator

The compensator (1) is a 2-position 2-way hydraulic operation actuator spring-actuated directional control valve. It is usually closed with the help of the spring. When the pressurised oil passing line A and reaches the compensator (1), without any signal, the compensator valve (1) is closed with the help of the spring. Then, pressurised fluid cannot pass the valve and cannot reach the tank [15]. The compensator only acts on the lifting module. The lowering module has no compensator. In fact, the lifting mechanism moves downwards using the weight of the implement and/or external forces such as the draft load. This system is modelled in MATLAB/Simulink. The maximum travel of the valve is 10 mm. The orifice opening are is computed as follows:

$$h = x_0 + x \tag{10}$$

Where h is the orifice opening, x_0 the initial opening, x control member displacement from initial position.

3.2.2 Modelling the lifting module

Lifting module (2) is a 2-position 3-way solenoid actuator spring-actuated direction a control valve. Typically, if an electrical signal is not given to the solenoid of the valve, pressurised fluid does not pass through the lifting module. If the electrical input is given to the solenoid, then the solenoid opens gradually according to the value of the given electrical signal current [15]. Meanwhile, lifting module solenoid takes the electrical signal only from lifting the current signal, which comes through controller. The characteristic curves of the lifting and lowering module are shown in **Figure 8**. The solenoid valve of the lifting module is initially closed with a stroke of 1 mm, and its maximum opening is 3.5 mm.

The orifice openings are computed separately for each flow path in terms of the respective opening offset:

$$\mathrm{h_{PA}} = \mathrm{h_{PA_0}} + \mathrm{x} \tag{11}$$

$$\mathrm{h_{AT}} = \mathrm{h_{AT_0}}\text{-}\mathrm{x} \tag{12}$$

where h_{PA} and h_{AT} are the orifice openings of the **P**-**A** and **A**-**T** flow paths. h_{PA0} and h_{AT0} are the opening offsets of the **P**-**A** and **A**-**T** flow paths. x is the spool displacement relative to what in the zero-offset case is a fully closed valve.

3.2.3 Modelling the lowering module

The logic of the lowering module (3) is almost similar to that of the lifting module. It is initially closed with a stroke of 1 mm, and its maximum opening is 3.5 mm.

The schematic diagram of a tractor's electrohydraulic lifting system is a closed-loop system (**Figure 9**). The first block is the operating unit, where control values are recorded. The red block is the tractor's electronic control unit. The control deviation resulting from the target/actual comparison is processed in the control unit and transmitted to the hitch control valve. The blue block contains the electrohydraulic actuator, where the hydraulic pump delivers a flow of oil to the hitch control valve, which in turn actuates the hitch cylinder. In the green block, the hitch cylinder acts on the lift arm so that implements can be lifted, held or lowered. The position sensor signal and the draft sensor are the feedback elements of the mechanism.

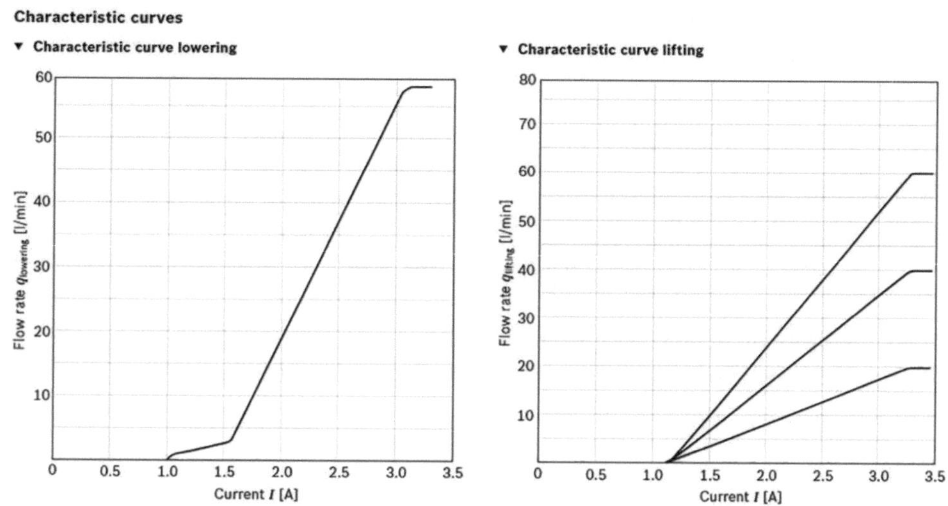

Figure 8.
Characteristic curves of the lifting and lowering modules [15].

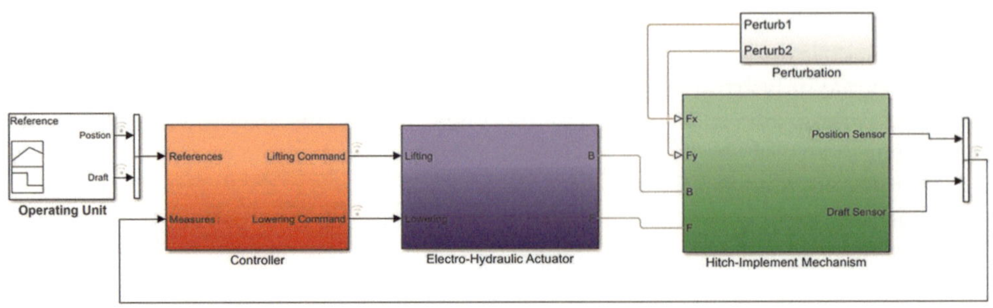

Figure 9.
Block diagram of the tillage depth control system.

4. Controller design

4.1 Mixed position-force control strategy

Position control involves adjusting the height of the implement above the ground, according to Eq. (13):

$$e = H_d - H_m \tag{13}$$

with e the depth deviation, H_d the desired depth and H_m the measured depth.

Force control consists of adjusting the height of the implement as a function of the draft load, using Eq. (13):

$$H_d = \frac{F}{T_s \times \left[a + b \times V + c \times V^2\right] \times W_e} \tag{14}$$

The depth deviation can be expressed using Eq. (13):

$$e = \frac{F_d - F_m}{T_s \times \left[a + b \times V + c \times V^2\right] \times W_e} \tag{15}$$

with e the depth deviation, F_d the desired force and F_m the measured force.

Here, the participation ratio of desired position and force is adjusted according to the mixing coefficient (M). The deviation in ploughing depth in mixed control can be written as follows:

$$e = \left(\frac{F_d - F_m}{T_s \times \left[a + b \times V + c \times V^2\right] \times W_e}\right) M + (H_d - H_m)(1 - M) \tag{16}$$

When the mixing coefficient M = 0, the system is in “position control” mode; when M = 1, the system is in “draft control” mode; when 0 < M < 1, the control mode is mixed.

4.2 Design of the neuro-fuzzy adaptive controller

The general architecture of the Adaptive Neuro-Fuzzy Inference System (ANFIS) comprises 5-layer neural network, where each layer corresponds to the realisation of a step in a Takagi Sugeno-type fuzzy inference system [16]. For simplicity, we assume that the fuzzy inference system has two inputs x and y, and z as its output (**Figure 10**).

The first layer enables the fuzzification of inputs x and y. Each neuron i in this layer corresponds to a linguistic variable. The inputs x and y are fuzzified using the membership functions of the linguistic variables A_i and B_i, (generally of triangular, trapezoidal or Gaussian form). Gaussian membership functions are defined by:

$$\mu_{A_i}(x) = \exp\left(-\frac{(x-c_i)^2}{2{a_i}^2}\right) \quad for \ i = 1, 2 \tag{17}$$

where c_i is the center and a_i the width of the membership function. These parameters are called "premises". The outputs of the first layer are as follows:

$$O_i^1 = \mu_{A_i}(x) \tag{18}$$

with $\mu_{A_i}(x)$ the degree of membership of the value x.

The second layer receives the output of each fuzzification node and calculates its output value using the product operator. This operator uses the derivability constraint to deploy the learning algorithm, with each node performing a fuzzy T-norm. The outputs of this layer are the rule weights, obtained by:

$$O_i^2 = w_i = \min\{\mu_{A_i}(x), \mu_{B_i}(y)\} \quad for \ i = 1, 2 \tag{19}$$

The third layer normalises the results provided by the previous layer. The results obtained represent the degree of involvement of the value in the final result.

$$O_i^3 = \overline{w_i} = \frac{w_i}{\sum_{i=1}^{2} w_i} \tag{20}$$

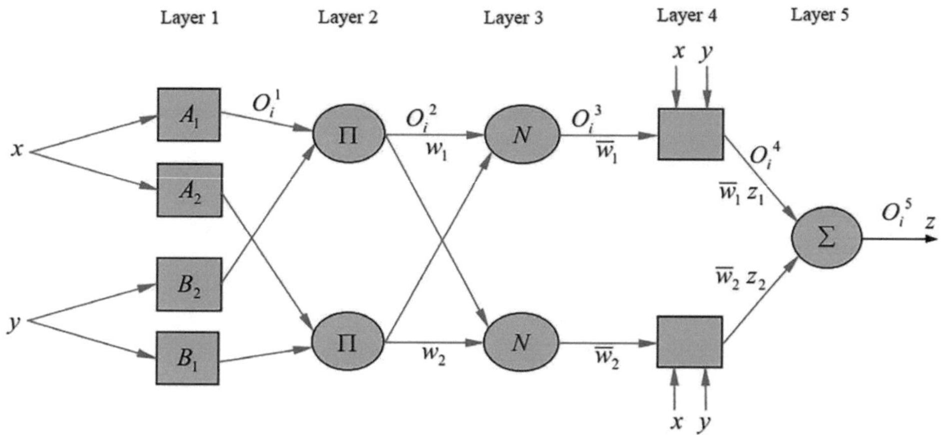

Figure 10.
ANFIS system architecture [16].

The fourth layer is linked to the initial inputs. The result is calculated as a function of its input and a first-order linear combination of the initial inputs (Takagi - Sugeno approach). This is the defuzzification phase.

$$O_i^4 = \overline{w_i} z_i = \overline{w_i} \times \left(p_i x + q_i y + r_i\right) \tag{21}$$

where $\overline{w_i}$ is the output of the third layer, p_i, q_i *et* r_i and are parameters referred to as: consequents.

The output layer consists of a single neuron that calculates the sum of the signals from the previous layer, so:

$$O_i^5 = \sum_{i=1}^{2} \overline{w_i} z_i \tag{22}$$

From the proposed architecture, we can see that there are two layers with adaptive parameters. Initially, the non-linear premises parameters (a_i, c_i) in layer 1, decide on the shape and position of the membership functions, and finally, the consequent parameters (p_i, q_i, r_i) realise a first-order linear combination of the initial inputs. These parameters are updated to minimise errors, using various learning algorithms like gradient descent only, Gradient descent and least-squares estimation (hybrid algorithm). In fact, the hybrid learning approach converges much faster than others. For this reason, it is this approach that we develop in the remainder of this work.

The MATLAB/Simulink environment was used to create, train and test the ANFIS model. First of all, the data for training and testing had to be loaded into the anfis editor. To this end, a PID controller is designed and applied to the system in order to obtain a set of input and output data for training. The parameters of the designed PID controller when the implement is lifted and when the implement is lowered are summarised in **Table 5**.

Before training in MATLAB/neurofuzzy, the data are divided into a three-dimensional vector, with 15% of the data set used for testing, 15% are used for verification, and 70% for training. Then, for the two inputs (e and ce), the initial membership functions are chosen. We then define the number of iterations and the desired learning error. Once these parameters have been defined, training can begin. Using a hybrid least-squares and back-propagation gradient descent algorithm method, MATLAB constructs a suitable Fuzzy Inference System (FIS). **Figure 11** shown he flowchart for the ANFIS method.

The hybrid algorithm performs a number of loops to minimise the error on the training data. A series of tests are carried out until an optimal architecture is obtained. The test results are summarised in **Table 6**.

After several trials and 20 iterations, a suitable neuro-fuzzy controller was obtained. The neuro-fuzzy controller obtained has seven Gaussian combination

Parameters	lifting	lowering
k_p	1,22	0,612
K_i	0	0
K_d	0	0,174

Table 5.
PID controller parameters.

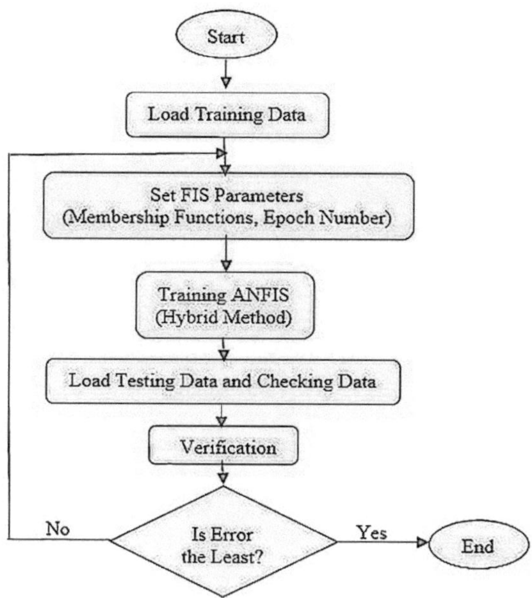

Figure 11.
Flowchart of the ANFIS method.

Membership function	Learning square error	Test square error	Number of iterations
Triangular	3.9%	4.4%	56
Trapezoidal	1.2%	1.9%	37
Gaussian	0.28%	0,31%	20
Gaussian2	0,28%	0,30%	80

Table 6.
Architectures obtained after various trials.

membership functions for the two inputs. After training, the error tolerance is close to zero. The membership functions obtained are shown in **Figure 12**.

The structure of the resulting neuro-fuzzy controller is shown in **Figure 13** with:

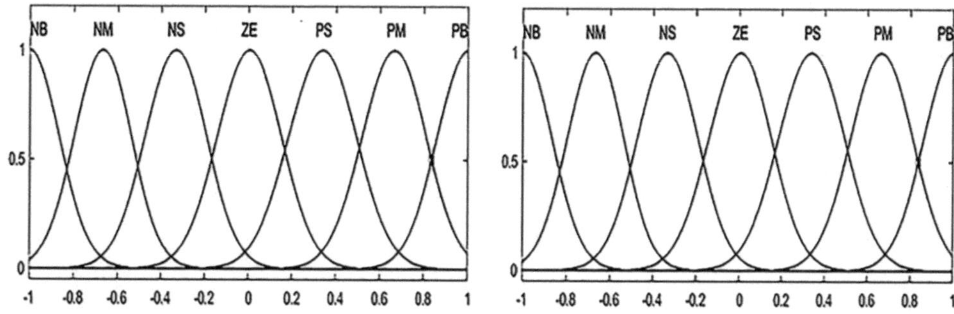

Figure 12.
Membership functions after learning.

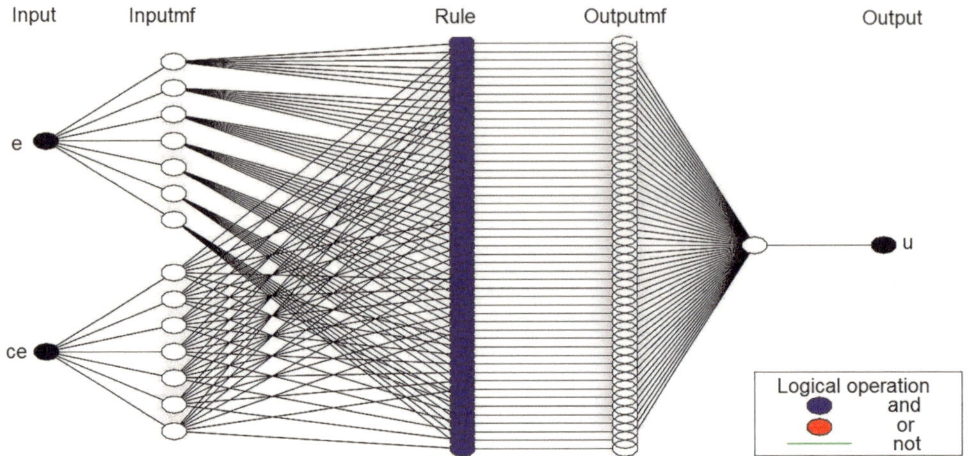

Figure 13.
Structure of the developed neuro-fuzzy controller.

- input: representing the two input variables (e) and (ce);
- inputmf: representing the membership functions of seven fuzzy sets for each input;
- rule: evokes and normalises the weights of the rules;
- outputmf: representing the defuzzification stage and the last layer gives the sum of all the data.

Figure 14 illustrates the principle of the proposed controller. The user enters the parameters of the desired depth Hd, the mixing coefficient M and the desired draft force Fd, from the operating unit. The signals from the force sensor and the position sensor are measured on the hitch mechanism and compared with the desired parameters. The 'mixing position and draft' module collects the above signals and uses Eq. (16), to calculate the deviation in depth e. From the deviation in depth e and its derivative ce, the 'neuro-fuzzy' module then sends the corresponding command value

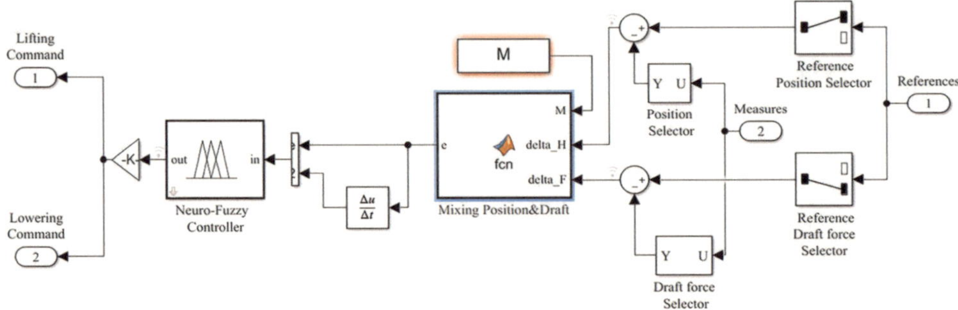

Figure 14.
Schematic diagram of the controller.

to the electrohydraulic valve which adjusts the working depth. To lift the implement, a positive signal is sent to the solenoid of the valve and the lifting valve control signal must be within an operating range of 1 to 3.35 A. A negative signal is sent to the solenoid of the valve to lower the implement, and the lowering valve control signal must be within an operating range of −1 to −3.35 A.

5. Analysis and interpretation of results

In this section, simulation tests are provided to show the effectiveness of the proposed neuro-fuzzy controller. The working depth errors during tillage operations with chisel and moldboard ploughs are examined. Chisel ploughs are designed for primary tillage with working depths of up to 45 cm. Moldboard ploughs are designed for soil tilth and seedbed preparation. Using the data in **Table 3**, the disturbance forces due to soil structure are of the order of $\pm 4048\ N$ for chisel plough, and for moldboard plough.

Simulation scenarios are carried out (**Figures 15–17**) on the chisel plough for different values of mix coefficient M, when the desired ploughing depth is 30 cm. **Figure 15** illustrates the variations around the desired working depth under PID and neuro-fuzzy control for M = 0. Between the instants t = 5 s and t = 55 s, the implement shows more variation around the desired working depth under PID control than under neuro-fuzzy control. This is due to the faster response of the neuro-fuzzy controller. Comparisons of the performance of the different controllers are summarised in **Table 7**. As shown in **Table 7**, ploughing depth error under neuro-fuzzy control has a maximum value of 0.85 cm. this value is significantly reduced compare to the PID controller, which indicate a maximum ploughing depth error value of 1.61 cm.

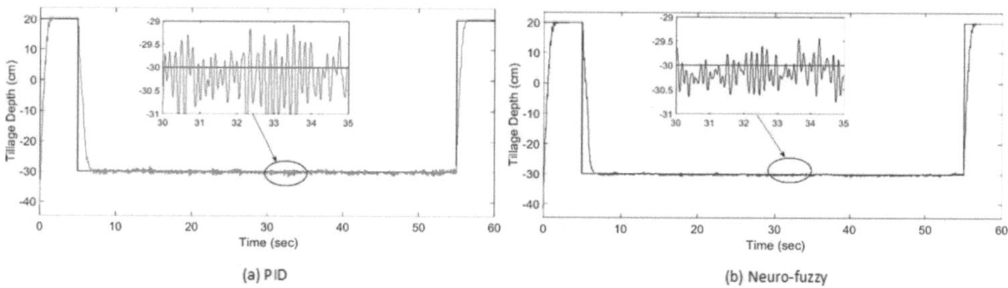

Figure 15.
Position of chisel plough for M = 0.

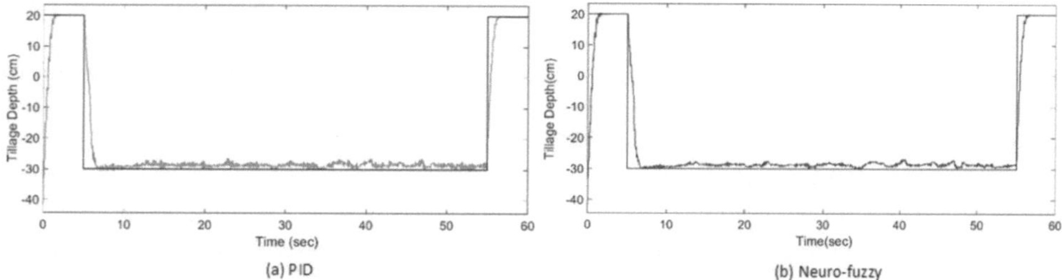

Figure 16.
Position of chisel plough for M = 0.25.

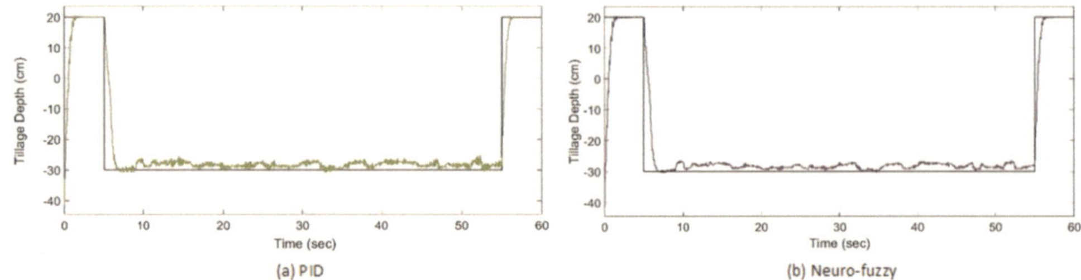

Figure 17.
Position of chisel plough for M = 0.5.

Implement	Controller	M value	Depth mean	min	max	Standard deviation	ITAE
Chisel plough	Neuro-fuzzy	M = 0	29.88	29.07	30.85	0.25	0.32
		M = 0.25	28.68	27.01	30.23	0.54	2.02
		M = 0.5	28.29	26.43	30.28	0.64	2.45
	PID	M = 0	29.47	28.92	31.61	0.45	0.76
		M = 0.25	27.96	26.9	30.70	0.77	2.27
		M = 0.5	27.67	26.22	30.96	0.78	2.71
Moldboard plough	Neuro-fuzzy	M = 0	9.94	9.66	10.18	0.09	0.11
		M = 0.25	9.84	9.51	10.23	0.11	0.41
		M = 0.5	9.69	9.23	10.08	0.17	0.65
	PID	M = 0	9.93	9.28	10.52	0.20	0.23
		M = 0.25	9.83	9.15	10.52	0.21	0.63
		M = 0.5	9.68	8.95	10.34	0.25	0.86

Table 7.
Performances of the different controllers.

Figure 16 shows the position of the chisel plough for M = 0.25. It can be seen that the ploughing depth errors increase. This is confirmed in the illustrations of **Figure 17**, where the ploughing errors are considerably greater. This can be justified by the fact that when the coefficient M increases, the controller takes into account the draft load as shown in Eq. (16), so the implement becomes more sensitive to soil resistance. This sensitivity is beneficial in limiting wheel slip, but the implement moves away from the desired depth when M > 0.5.

Figure 18 shows the variations around the desired working depth (10 cm) of the mouldboard plough under PID control, for M = 0, M = 0.25, and M = 0.5. We note that there is no significant variation as the M coefficient increases. This is due to the fact that, at shallow ploughing depths, soil resistances are reduced. **Figure 19** illustrates the positions of the mouldboard plough under neuro-fuzzy control. With reference to **Table 7**, for moldboard plough, the minimal standard deviation in ploughing depth was obtained in the cases of the neuro-fuzzy control. This leads to the conclusion that, whatever the

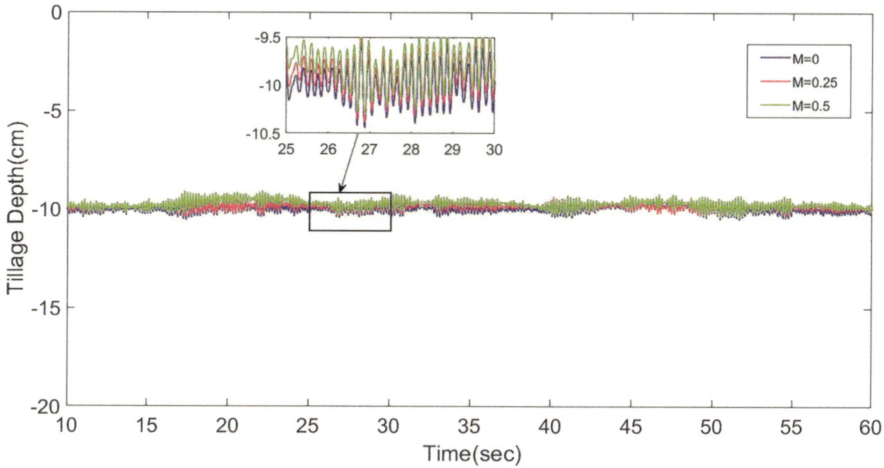

Figure 18.
Moldboard plough position under PID control.

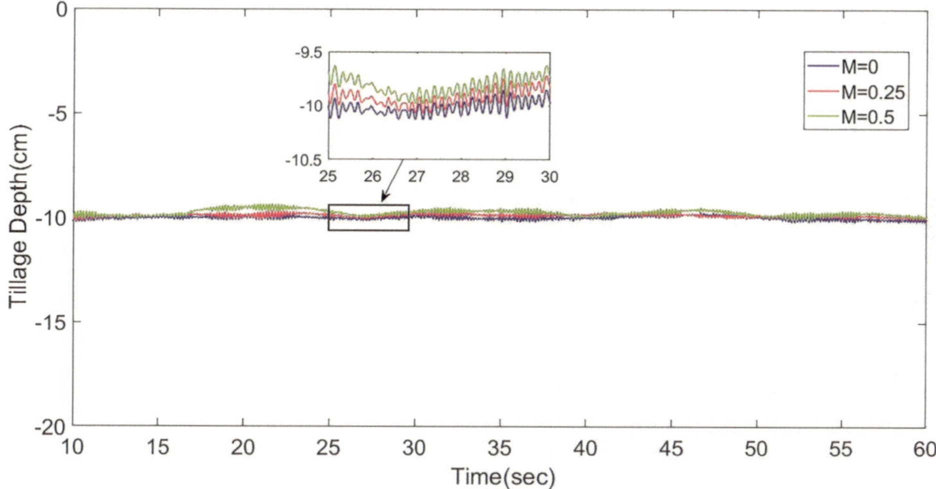

Figure 19.
Moldboard plough position under neuro-fuzzy control.

type of implement used, the neuro-fuzzy controller offers a faster response and enables the implement to follow the desired working depth more accurately.

In this work, we use the Integral Time Absolute value Error (ITAE) criterion, to evaluate the proposed neuro-fuzzy controller. We consider the ITAE criterion defined by:

$$ITAE = \int_0^\infty t|e(t)|dt \quad (23)$$

As shown in **Table 7** the ITAE values of the neuro-fuzzy controller are lower than those obtained by the PID controller. The average working depth values reported in **Table 7** indicate that the neuro fuzzy controller considerably reduced ploughing

Reference	Controller	Implement	Depth mean	Standard deviation
Han et al. [3]	Fuzzy	—	99,33%	0,66
Shafaei et al. [4]	Fuzzy	Moldboard plough	85,05%	0,78
		Chisel plough	89,17%	0,87
Current study	Neuro-fuzzy	Moldboard plough	99,6%	0,25
		Chisel plough	99,4%	0,11

Table 8.
Comparison with previous works.

errors. From the observations below, we can conclude that the system offers a great robustness against perturbations and a better stability using the neuro-fuzzy controller rather than the PID controller.

The results obtained in this work are compared with those obtained in the literature. Indeed, this problem is addressed by the authors using a fuzzy logic controller on the tractor's electro-hydraulic lifting system. These results are reproduced here and compared with the results found by the Neuro-fuzzy controller (**Table 8**).

6. Conclusion

This chapter gives detailed information about the design of an adaptive neuro-fuzzy controller for the tractor's electro-hydraulic lifting system. Mainly, it focusses on the modelling and analysis of the hitch-implement mechanism, modelling of the hydraulic system, controller design, and simulations of the overall system. On the tractor's electro-hydraulic lifting system, changes in hydraulic cylinder thrust impose changes in working depth values. The results of the selected scenarios showed that the proposed neuro-fuzzy controller can achieve the desired working depth even under disturbing effects with different ploughing depths and implements. However, the effect of applying the neuro-fuzzy controller for ploughing operations on fuel consumption, drive wheel slip, energy efficiency and forward speed was not analysed in this work. These parameters should be taken into account in future work. In addition, to improve the accuracy of the tractor's electrohydraulic lifting system, control of hydraulic pump pressure and flow rate should become a future trend.

Conflict of interest

The authors declare that there is no conflict of interests regarding the publication of this chapter.

Author details

Aristide Timene[1*], Ndjiya Ngasop[2] and Haman Djalo[1]

1 Faculty of Sciences, Department of Physics, University of Ngaoundere, Cameroon

2 Department of Electrical Engineering, Energy and Automation, National School of Agro-Industrial Sciences, University of Ngaoundere, Cameroon

*Address all correspondence to: aristidetimene@yahoo.com

References

[1] Bhondave B, Ganesan T, Varma N, Renu R, Sabarinath N. Design and development of electro hydraulics hitch control for agricultural tractor. SAE International Journal of Commercial Vehicles. 2017;**10**:405-410

[2] Suomi P, Oksanen T. Automatic working depth control for seed drill using ISO 11783 remote control messages. Computers and Electronic in Agriculture. 2015;**116**:30-35

[3] Han J, Xia C, Shang G, Gao X. In-field experiment of electro-hydraulic tillage depth draft-position mixed control on tractor. IOP Conference Series: Materials Science and Engineering. 2017;**274**

[4] Shafaei SM, Loghavi M, Kamgar S. A practical effort to equip tractor-implement with fuzzy depth and draft control system. Engineering in Agriculture Environment and Food. 2019;**12**:191-203

[5] Subha S, Nagalakshmi S. Design of ANFIS controller for intelligent energy management in smart grid applications. Journal of Ambient Intelligence and Humanized Computing. 2020;**11**(n 6): 1-11

[6] Shanthi R, Kalyani S, Devie et PM . Design and performance analysis of adaptive neuro-fuzzy controller for speed control of permanent magnet synchronous motor drive. Soft Computing. 2021;**25**(n 2): 1519-1533

[7] Saadat SA et al. Adaptive neuro-fuzzy inference systems (ANFIS) controller design on single-phase full-bridge inverter with a cascade fractional-order PID voltage controller. IET Power Electronics. 2021;**14**:1960-1972

[8] Oladipo S, Sun Y. Enhanced adaptive neuro-fuzzy inference system using genetic algorithm: A case study in predicting electricity consumption. SN Applied Sciences. 2023;**5**:186

[9] Bentaher H, Hamza E, Kantchev G, Maalej A, Arnold W. Three point hitch mechanism instrumentation for tillage power optimization. Biosystems Engineering. 2008;**100**:24-30

[10] International Organization for Standardization. GOST ISO 730-2019 Agricultural Wheeled Tractors-Rear Mounted Three-Point Linkage - Categories 1N, 1, 2, 3N, 3, 4N and 4. Geneva; 2020

[11] Attachment TF, Implements H, Tractors AW. ASAE S217.12 three-point free-link attachment for hitching implements to agricultural wheel tractors. Power. 2001;**1**

[12] University of Nebraska. Nebraska Tractor Test Laboratory, Nebraska Summary: S706 Massey Ferguson 5460. Lincoln, Nebraska: University of Nebraska; 2009

[13] Standards ASAE. Agricultural machinery management data. ASAE. 2020;**D497**:7

[14] Cad FKG, Plaza EC. Fulltrac Fluid X10W-30 High Protection for Transmissions of Tractor and Agricultural Machines. Istanbul; 2021. Available from: https: //www.opetfuchs.com.tr/content/pdf/tds_fulltrac_X_10w30

[15] Bosch Rexroth AG. Hitch Control Valves EHR5-OC, EHR5-LS, EHR23-EM2 RE. 2020. Available from: https://

www.naptechniek.nl/images/catalogus/pdf/EHR23_re66125_2013-07.pdf

[16] Jang JS. ANFIS: Adaptive-network-based fuzzy inference system. IEEE Transactions on Systems, Man, and Cybernetics. 1993;**23**(3):665-685

Chapter 3

Solar Radiation Prediction Using an Improved Adaptive Neuro-Fuzzy Inference System (ANFIS) Optimization Ensemble

Ammar Muhammad Ibrahim, Salisu Muhammad Lawan, Rabiu Abdulkadir, Nazifi Sani Shuaibu, Muhammad Uzair, Musbahu Garba Indabawa, Masud Ibrahim and Abdullahi Mahmoud Aliyu

Abstract

A dependable design and monitoring of solar energy-based systems necessitates precise data on available solar radiation. However, measuring solar radiation is challenging due to the expensive equipment required for measurement, along with the costs of calibration and maintenance, especially in developing countries like Nigeria. As a result, data-driven techniques are often employed to predict solar radiation in such regions. However, the existing predictive models frequently yield unsatisfactory outcomes. To address this issue, this study proposes the creation of intelligent models to forecast solar radiation in Kano state, Nigeria. The model is developed using an ensemble machine learning approach that combines two Adaptive Neuro-Fuzzy Inference Systems with sub-clustering optimization and grid-partitioning optimization. The meteorological data used for model development include maximum temperature, minimum temperature, mean temperature, and solar radiation from the previous 2 days as predictors. To evaluate the model's performance, various metrics like correlation coefficient, determination coefficient, mean-squared error, root-mean-squared error, and mean-absolute error are employed. The simulation results demonstrate that the ANFIS ensemble outperforms the individual ANFIS models. Notably, the ANFIS-ENS exhibits the highest accuracy. Consequently, the developed models provide a reliable alternative for estimating solar radiation in Kano and can be instrumental in enhancing the design and management of solar energy systems in the region.

Keywords: solar radiation, prediction, ANFIS, Kano state, Nigeria

1. Introduction

Energy is the most important input for economic development of any country. The demand for energy in countries has grown extensively owing to the rise in industrial sector, technological advancement, and increase in population. However, developing countries such as Nigeria have inadequate energy resources to address the need for energy. The swift increase in energy consumption pushes some countries to look for alternative forms of energy sources. The renewable energy (RE) has essentially contributed to energy output portfolio, its increasing in compared to other fossil fuels such as coal, natural gas, and petroleum [1–7]. It includes solar, wind, hydro, hydrogen, biomass, tidal energy and geothermal [8]. In electricity generation, solar energy plays a vital role increasingly, it has become one of the most encouraging RE sources and perhaps calls the attention of countries for being free to access, clean, endless, and continuous in comparison with fossil fuel. Due to this, recent contribution of solar energy for electricity generation is accelerating so quickly besides advancement in solar energy technology, over-reliance on other countries, universal climate change, and other environmental factors [9, 10].

For electricity generation, photovoltaic (PV) system has been used reliably more than 40 years ago and the amount of energy produced is at least 480GW [11]. Nevertheless, prior to designing and modelling of PV system for a certain geographical area, the utilization of PV is limited due to the design challenges solar radiation (SR) data must be recorded. The possibility of the design could be evaluated using SR data. Besides PV design, SR data find application in many scientific and engineering solar works [12]. Due to this, acquiring long-term data for a specific geographical location is the most precise method. However, it is also impossible to measure SR everywhere because it is a costly, long, and accurate process. Additionally, because measurement of radiation values can only be in peculiar areas, values of radiation cannot be measured in precise way for so many countries. To obtain the SR globally statistical, experimental and artificial intelligence-based predictive models were established [8, 13, 14]. Machine Language (ML), which is a subfield of AI, was one of the familiar methods deployed in predictive studies.

Predicting PV electricity production significantly assists in overcoming this barrier by facilitating grid management through planning and maintenance. Researchers have developed a variety of methods to achieve this goal [15]. Forecasting PV electricity production plays a crucial role in overcoming barriers related to grid management, planning, and maintenance. Various methods have been developed by researchers to achieve this objective [16]. The existing literature categorizes solar prediction methods into three groups: short-term prediction, medium-term prediction, and long-term prediction. Additionally, to accurately predict solar radiation, four different models have been identified in the literature: physical models, empirical models, machine learning models, and statistical models. Physical models, such as sky view-based models, establish the relationship between solar radiation (SR) and other meteorological parameters based on a solid physical foundation. However, the complexity of atmospheric conditions makes the structure of physical models intricate. On the other hand, empirical models utilize linear or nonlinear regression equations to forecast solar radiation. While simple and user-friendly, their accuracy is often limited. Statistical models, including the autoregressive moving-average model (ARMA) and the autoregressive integrated moving-average model (ARIMA), are developed based on statistical correlations. They tend to be more accurate than empirical models, but they struggle to capture nonlinear correlations between SR and other parameters.

Machine learning models, such as artificial neural networks (ANNs), support vector machines (SVMs), and adaptive neural-fuzzy inference systems (ANFIS), outperform empirical, physical, and statistical models in both accuracy and application. Among these, ANN models like multilayer perceptron (MLP) and radial basis function network (RBFN) are commonly used and have demonstrated moderate accuracy in predicting short-term, medium-term, and long-term SR [17]. The fourth category consists of hybrid models, which combine two or more methods to enhance forecasting accuracy. Hybrid models draw on the strengths of each method, resulting in improved overall performance. Several hybrid models combining machine learning algorithms, physical models, mathematical methods, and optimization algorithms have been proposed in the literature [16]. These hybrid models generally outperform individual methods in terms of prediction accuracy. However, they come with a drawback of high computational complexity, demanding significant time and space resources to execute. Moreover, their performance heavily relies on the careful selection of historical inputs [18]. Machine learning (ML) models have garnered considerable attention from researchers due to their exceptional prediction accuracy and user-friendly nature. In a study conducted by [19], they explored the transferability of Support Vector Machines (SVM) in predicting solar radiation (SR) based on temperature data. Their findings indicated that SVM could indeed be employed effectively for SR prediction. Additionally, they observed that factors like the distance between two locations and diurnal temperature range influenced the accuracy of SVM predictions. Guermoui et al. [20] presented a temperature-based corrected SVM model for estimating SR. This novel approach involved combining an SVM model for SR prediction with another SVM model for SR error estimation, leading to enhanced SVM performance. In a different study, [21] Linares-Rodriguez et al. utilized satellite irradiances to predict SR in Spain using the Multilayer Perceptron (MLP) model. The MLP model demonstrated excellent performance in both clear and cloudy sky conditions. Sözen et al. [22] estimated solar radiation in Turkey using an Artificial Neural Network (ANN) model, incorporating geographical and meteorological data as input variables. Their MLP network achieved a Mean Absolute Percentage Error (MAPE) of 6.73%, showcasing its accuracy in predicting solar radiation levels.

ANFIS has been widely utilized in numerous recent studies for solar radiation (SR) prediction, employing different input variables. For instance, Piri and Kisi [23] developed an ANFIS model with humidity, sunshine, and temperature data as inputs. Benmouiza and Cheknane [24] created hybrid models by integrating ANFIS with various clustering algorithms like grid partitioning, fuzzy c-means (FCM), and subtractive clustering to forecast hourly solar radiation in Algeria. Mohammadi et al. [25] utilized the ANFIS approach to identify the most crucial input parameters for SR prediction, concluding that temperature played a critical role. Naderloo [26] predicted daily solar radiation using both ANN and ANFIS models, with meteorological factors like temperature, relative humidity, and precipitation as inputs. The ANN model produced slightly superior results when compared to ANFIS. In another study, Wang et al. [27] employed ANFIS with grid partitioning and subtractive clustering (ANFIS-SC and ANFIS-GP), utilizing pressure, sunlight, humidity, and temperature data as inputs. Nourani et al. [28] estimated daily global solar radiation in Iraq using various meteorological parameters and compared classical model MLR with various AI methods, including ANFIS. The ANFIS method outperformed other predictive models in terms of accuracy. Sthitapragyan et al. [29] estimated the monthly mean global solar radiation in three different regions in Eastern India using ANFIS, Radial Basis Function (RBF), and Multi-layer Perceptron (MLP) methods. Among the three, the ANFIS method showed significantly successful results compared to the meteorological data. A comparison of different AI models for SR prediction demonstrated that the ANFIS method is particularly suitable for SR estimation due to its capability to account for the uncertainty associated with time-series data [30].

In contemporary research on soft computing and computational methods, a cutting-edge approach has emerged, involving the integration of distinct machine learning models into an ensemble framework to synergistically enhance their performance. The effectiveness of ensemble machine learning techniques has been demonstrated across various modeling applications [31–34]. Thus, the current study aims to leverage this ensemble methodology for estimating solar radiation levels. By applying the ensemble method to solar radiation estimation, we seek to capitalize on the strengths of multiple models, thereby potentially improving the accuracy and reliability of solar radiation forecasts.

In this research endeavor, we have developed an advanced ANFIS ensemble model, which harmoniously incorporates the ANFIS Grid Partition (ANFIS-GP) and ANFIS Subtractive Clustering (ANFIS-SC) methodologies. By leveraging the unique strengths of these two ANFIS variants, our approach aims to enhance the precision and robustness of solar radiation estimation. This innovative ensemble model holds significant promise as a valuable tool for accurate and reliable solar energy prediction. The integration of ANFIS-GP and ANFIS-SC enables us to effectively capture complex relationships inherent in solar radiation data, paving the way for informed decision-making processes within the renewable energy domain. Our research findings highlight the potential impact of this advanced model in advancing the state-of-the-art in solar radiation forecasting and supporting sustainable energy management practices.

2. Material and method

The step-by-step procedure of the entire study is illustrated in the flow chart, as shown in **Figure 1**. Our approach introduces three distinct ANFIS models. The first model is trained using the grid-partitioning optimization method (ANFIS-GP), while the second model adopts the sub clustering optimization technique (ANFIS-SC). To maximize the benefits of these optimization approaches, we create a third model by combining them in an ensemble manner (ANFIS-ENS). This ensemble configuration allows us to leverage the unique strengths of each model.

The subsequent sections elaborate on how we collected and preprocessed the data, along with the evaluation procedure used to measure the performance of our developed models. By following this comprehensive methodology, we aim to achieve accurate and reliable estimations of solar radiation.

The methodology is succinctly outlined in **Figure 1** above and can be elaborated upon in greater detail below:

2.1 Data collection and preprocessing

In this research, we collected a dataset containing daily solar radiation parameters for the entire year of 2018, spanning from January to December. The parameters consist of maximum temperature (Tmax), minimum temperature (Tmin), average temperature (T), and solar radiations (SR_k, SR_{k-1}, SR_{k-2}). The study location, Kano, is positioned at a latitude of 12°03′N and a longitude of 12°32′E, with an altitude of approximately 472 meters above sea level. The average height of the study area is around 472.45 meters. To acquire the data, we obtained information from the Nigerian Meteorological Agency (NIMET). The original dataset encompassed various parameters, including average temperature (T), maximum temperature (Tmax), minimum temperature (Tmin), precipitation (R), wind speed (WS), relative

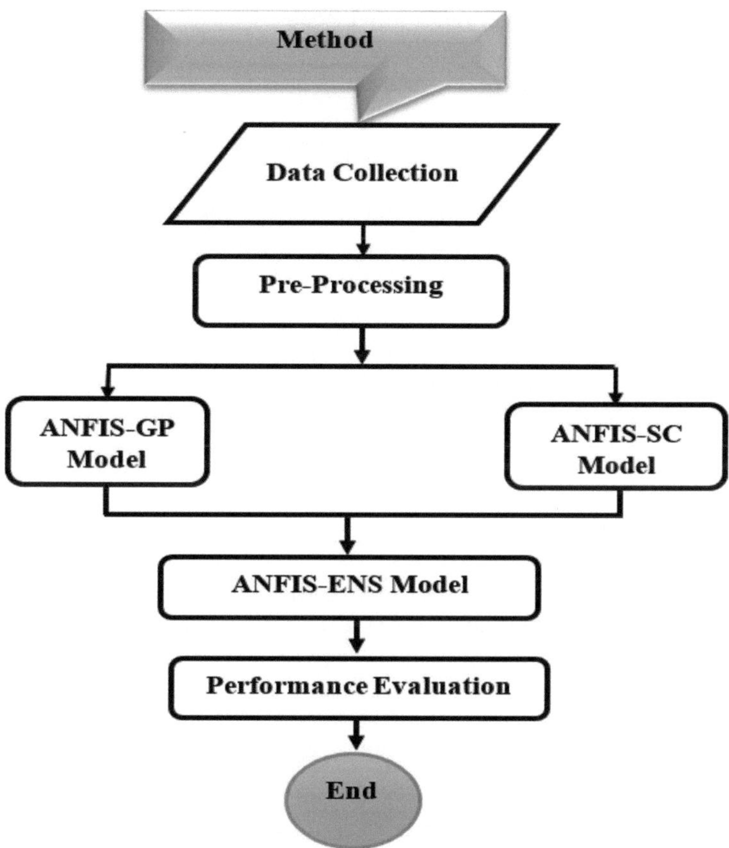

Figure 1.
Proposed methodology.

humidity (RH), and solar radiation (SR). To ensure an optimal model, we evaluated the correlations between these parameters and selected those with a correlation greater than or equal to 50%. This approach helps avoid including irrelevant parameters that may not significantly impact the output. **Figure 2** illustrates the correlation matrix, revealing a high correlation between var7 (representing solar radiation) and the first three variables, var1, var2, and var3 (representing mean, maximum, and minimum temperatures, respectively). Consequently, we only utilized these three variables for our modeling purposes.

In the context of our study, we have formulated a comprehensive model that incorporates a range of predictors, including mean, maximum, and minimum temperatures, along with solar radiation data from the preceding 2 days. This mathematical representation elegantly captures the interplay of these factors, empowering us to make accurate predictions and draw insightful conclusions. This is expressed mathematically as in Eq. (1) below:

$$M1 = SR_k(T, Tmax, Tmin, SR_{k-1}, SR_{k-2}) \tag{1}$$

where M1 represents the developed model and SR_k denotes the solar radiation to be predicted or the output of the model. The inputs of the model include:

- T, which represents the average temperature.
- Tmax, which signifies the maximum temperature.
- Tmin, which denotes the minimum temperature.
- SR_{k-1} *and* SR_{k-2} representing the solar radiations for the preceding 2 days.

2.2 ANFIS-GP and ANFIS-SC

This section of the methodology involves the development of individual models, ANFIS-SC and ANFIS-GP, takes place. During this stage, the processed data is utilized for model development, with 70% of the data allocated for training, while the remaining 30% is designated for testing in each of the two models.

2.3 ANFIS-ENS model

This section of the methodology pertains to the ANFIS-ENS model. In this section, the strength of the individual models is combined. By doing so, ANFIS-ENS can harness its complementary capabilities to enhance overall accuracy.

2.4 Performance evaluation

The final section of the methodology involves performance evaluation. In this section, the accuracy of the model is scrutinized using a range of diverse performance metrics, this can be explained in Section 2.7 of the chapter.

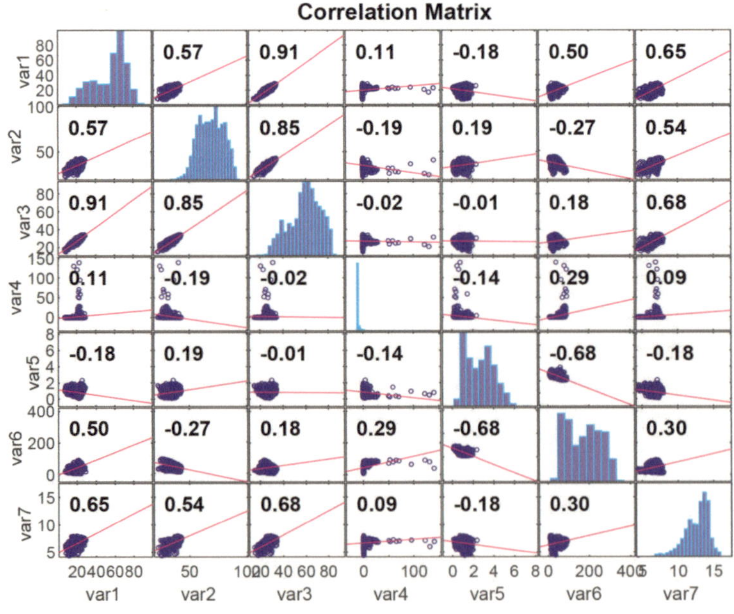

Figure 2.
Correlation matrix.

2.5 Adaptive neuro-fuzzy inference system (ANFIS)

The Adaptive Neuro-Fuzzy Inference System (ANFIS) is a powerful amalgamation of fuzzy logic and the learning capabilities of neural networks [35]. ANFIS encompasses three primary types: Mamdani, Sugeno, and Tsumoto, with Sugeno's system being the most widely utilized [27, 36, 37]. In Fuzzy logic, input data are transformed into fuzzy values through the application of membership functions, where fuzzy values range from 0 to 1. The ANFIS model's structure is formed by nodes functioning as membership functions (MFs) and rules that define the relationship between input and output. Various types of membership functions are available, including triangular, trapezoidal, Gaussian, and sigmoid. Among these, the Gaussian function (as shown in Eq. (4) below) is commonly employed [38].

$$\mathrm{V_{Li}} = \frac{1}{1 + \left[\left(X^{-\alpha i} \right) / \beta i \right]^{2\mu i}} \tag{2}$$

The input variable x corresponds to the i node, where VLi represents the membership function, and βi and μi serve as the conditional parameters of this function. In the ANFIS framework, rules are formulated based on their antecedents (the "if" part) and consequents (the "then" part), and these rules are stored in a fuzzy-based rule system referred to as "the IF-THEN" rules. The rules for a Sugeno ANFIS model with two inputs (a and b) and one output f are illustrated by Eq. (5) and (6) [39].

$$\textit{Rule } 1; \textit{If } x \textit{ is } P_1 \textit{ and } y \textit{ is } Q_1, \textit{then} f_1 = P_1 x + q_1 y + r_1 \tag{3}$$

$$\textit{Rule } 2; \textit{If } x \textit{ is } P_2 \textit{ and } y \textit{ is } Q_2 \textit{ then} f_2 = P_2 x + q_2 x + r_2 \tag{4}$$

P_1, P_2, ***is*** Q_1, and ***is*** Q_2 are referred to as fuzzy sets, while f_1 and f_2 represent the output within the fuzzy region. The design parameters, r_1 and r_2, are derived during the training process. The architecture of an ANFIS with two inputs (x and y) and one output (f) is depicted in **Figure 3a**. An elaborate investigation into ANFIS is presented by Mature et al. [27]. The goal is to minimize the objective function, as illustrated in **Figure 4**, before computing new fuzzy clusters. The fuzzifier exponent, P, lies

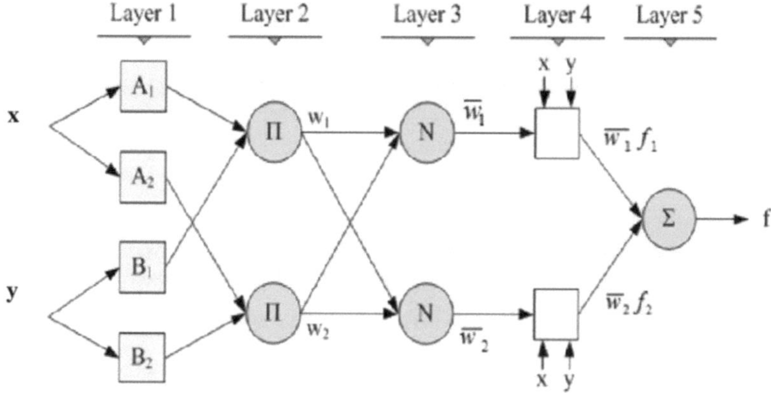

Figure 3.
ANFIS structure with two inputs, one output, and two rules [40].

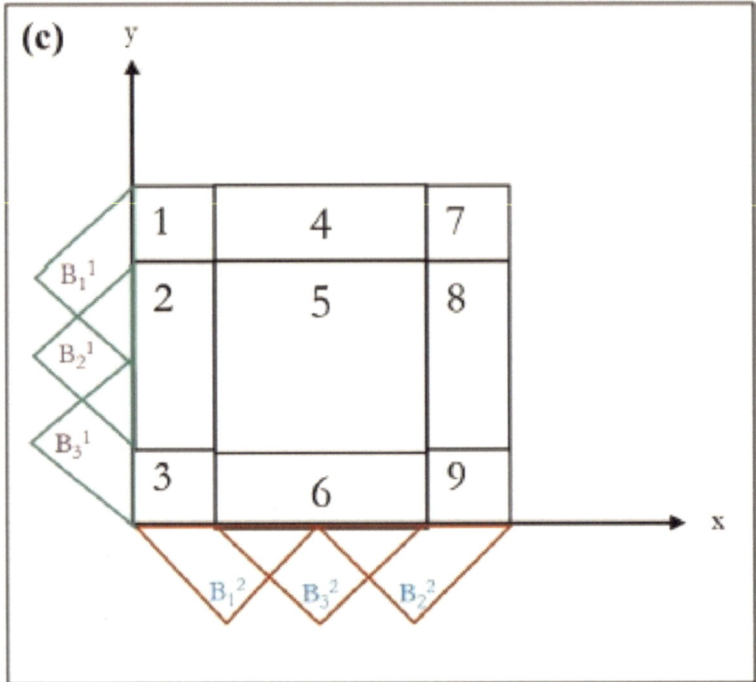

Figure 4.
Grid partitioning having 2 inputs with k = 3 [42].

between 0 and 1, while c represents the number of clusters. N denotes the number of data points, and a signifies the cluster centers.

In general, ANFIS comprises five distinct layers, illustrated in **Figure 1**, which are denoted as follows: the input layer, the layer for membership functions, the fuzzification layer, the defuzzification layer, and the normalization layer. This system operates with two inputs, specifically referred to as "x" and "y." In this context, A1 and B1 represent fuzzy sets, while p1, q1, and r1 are design parameters, where i takes on values of 1 and 2.

The first layer within the ANFIS structure is the membership layer. In this layer, all nodes are adaptive, and it is responsible for generating membership grades for each input. This functionality is represented in equation above.

Moving on to the subsequent layer, it involves straightforward multiplication and is composed of fixed nodes. The mathematical representation of this layer can be expressed as follows:

$$O_{2,i} = w_i = \mu_{Ai}(x) \times \mu_{Bi}(x) \; i = 1, 2 \tag{5}$$

In the subsequent layer, there is a fixed node dedicated to normalization. This layer is responsible for standardizing the output generated by the second layer. The operation can be illustrated using the following equation:

$$O_{3,i} = \overline{w} = \frac{w_i}{w_1 + w_2} \; i = 1, 2 \tag{6}$$

In this context, the firing level of node "i" is represented by $w_{i.}$

The fourth layer has the ability to streamline the result of the normalized output from the third layer. This layer adjusts itself dynamically, and you can express its output using the following equation:

$$O_{4,i} = \overline{w}f_i = \overline{w_i}\left(p_1 + q_1 + r_1\right) i = 1, 2 \tag{7}$$

The last layer consists of a single fixed node, responsible for summing all incoming inputs. Ultimately, you can represent the overall result using the following equation:

$$O_{5,i} = \sum_{i=1}^{2} \overline{w}f_i = \frac{w_1 f_1 + w_2 f_2}{w_1 + w_2} \tag{8}$$

ANFIS exhibits improved learning capabilities due to the incorporation of back propagation and least square methods, which improve the system's accuracy and expedite convergence. As previously mentioned, there are six consequent parameters in this system when assuming the utilization of bell-shaped membership functions. The primary goal within this ANFIS system is to optimize these parameters to achieve the lowest cost. Specifically, back propagation is employed to modify the parameters in the first layer, while the least square approach is responsible for fine-tuning the parameters in the fourth layer [41].

2.5.1 Grid partitioning (GP)

In ANFIS-GP, the integration of ANFIS and grid-partitioning techniques is employed. The grid-partitioning method involves dividing the data into smaller subsets, referred to as grid data, based on the type of membership function (MFS) in each dimension. The chart representation of ANFIS-GP, with three partitions (k = 3), is depicted in **Figure 3b**. Initially, ANFIS-GP starts with zero output and gradually learns distinct fuzzy set rules and functions through the training process [27]. To determine the initial fuzzy sets and parameters, the least square method is utilized, considering the partitions and MF types [43].

2.5.2 Subtractive clustering (SC)

The integration of ANFIS and SC yields ANFIS-SC. Each individual data point is considered a possible cluster center. As a result, a point surrounded by multiple neighboring points exhibits a higher potential value. To identify the first cluster center, a density measure (d_i) is defined in Eq. (9) below, and the data set point with the highest density or potential value is selected as the initial cluster center [44].

$$d_i = \sum_{K=1}^{N} \boldsymbol{exp}\left(-\left(\frac{2}{r_0}\right)^2 . \|x_i - x_k\|^2\right) \tag{9}$$

The data point x_i is regarded as the cluster center, while x_k represents the remaining data points within the influence radius, which is used to determine the initial cluster center. To calculate the new density measurement, Eq. (10) below is utilized [45].

$$d_{inew} = d_i - d'_1.\boldsymbol{exp}\left(-\frac{\left(-\|x_i - x'_1\|^2\right)}{\left(\frac{r_b}{2}\right)^2}\right) \quad (10)$$

The constant value r_b defines the neighborhood range within which the potential will steadily decrease. Subsequent data points after the first cluster center experience a significant decrease in potential and become less likely to be chosen as subsequent cluster centers. Selecting the appropriate influential radius is crucial as it determines the number of clusters. The optimal value for r_a should fall within the range of 0.1 to 2 [46], and specifically, r_a equals 1.25 times r_b [47]. Larger clusters will result in the development of more rules, making it important to avoid very small radii. Therefore, careful consideration in choosing the influential radius is vital for effective clustering.

2.6 Ensemble machine learning

Ensemble machine learning emerges as a valuable approach to address the varying levels of accuracy exhibited by individual models, owing to their distinct robustness and constraints. This diversity of performance may lead to unsatisfactory outcomes in certain cases. Consequently, the adoption of ensemble techniques has become widespread across diverse fields, encompassing science, engineering, social and management sciences, health sciences, and beyond [17]. Ensemble methods involve the combination of both heterogeneous and homogeneous models, effectively harnessing their collective predictive power. Instead of relying solely on standalone models, ensemble techniques integrate the individual outputs of these models as new input variables, aiming to enhance the final performance skills of the simple models. Numerous empirical studies have consistently demonstrated that ensemble approaches yield superior results, particularly when confronted with complex and intricate problems. By leveraging the advantages of ensemble machine learning, practitioners can significantly elevate the reliability and efficacy of their solutions, providing robust and accurate solutions to multifaceted challenges. Embracing the potential of ensemble methods opens up new possibilities for advancing predictive modeling and decision-making processes across various domains. In this research, the ensemble model, ANFIS-ENS, combines the strengths of the individual models known as ANFIS-GP and ANFIS-SC. By combining these two paradigms, the ensemble can take advantage of their complementary capabilities and thus enhance the overall performance of the model.

Above is a block diagram of the developed model. The processed inputs of the model, T, Tmax, Tmin, SR_{K-1}, and SR_{K-2}, are trained using the individual models. Within each of these individual models, solar radiation is predicted, and the output is obtained. The outputs of the individual models, ANFIS-GP and ANFIS-SC, are now used as inputs for the Meta model known as ANFIS-ENS.

2.7 Performance evaluation

The evaluation of model performance throughout both training and testing stages involves the utilization of four widely recognized statistical metrics: the correlation coefficient (R), determination coefficient (DC), mean-squared-error (MSE), root-mean-squared-error (RMSE), and mean absolute error (MAE). These essential metrics provide valuable insights into the models' predictive accuracy, enabling a comprehensive assessment of their efficacy and generalization capabilities. The computation of these metrics is facilitated by employing Eq. (11)–(13) [48–50].

2.7.1 Pearson correlation coefficient (R)

The Pearson correlation coefficient is a measure that evaluates the magnitude or strength and direction of the linear relationship between two variables. It signifies the extent to which one variable changes when the other variable changes, and is expressed as numerical value between −1 and 1 [18].

A Pearson correlation coefficient of −1 signifies a perfect negative linear relationship, which means that when one variable decreases, the other variable increases in a linear fashion. A Pearson correlation coefficient of +1 signifies a superb positive linear relationship between the two variables, which means that when one variable increases, the other variable also increases in a linear fashion. A Pearson correlation coefficient of 0 indicates no linear relationship between the two variables. The Pearson correlation coefficient can be computed by the following equation:

$$R = \frac{\sum((x_i - \overline{x}) - (y_i - \overline{y}))}{\sqrt{\sum (x_i - \overline{x})^2 \sum (y_i - y)^?}} \tag{11}$$

Where x_i is independent variable, y_i is dependent variable, $\overline{x}$ is the mean of variable x_i values, and $\overline{y}$ is the mean of variable y_i values.

2.7.2 Coefficient of determination (DC)

Coefficient of determination, also known as R-squared, is a statistical metric that evaluates how effectively a regression model fits the data points [13]. It is a value ranging from 0 to 1 that symbolizes the proportion of the variance in the dependent variable that can be predicted from the independent variable(s). A DC value of 1 represents a perfect fit of the regression predictions, while a DC value of 0 suggests that the model does not account for any of the dependent variable's variation. A higher DC value indicates a better fit of the model to the data, moreover, DC is calculated as the ratio of the explained variance to the total variance. The explained variance is the variation in the dependent variable that is explained by the independent variable(s), while the total variance is the variation in the dependent variable that is not explained by the independent variable(s). Below is the mathematical expression for DC:

$$DC = 1 - \frac{\sum (x_i - \widehat{x}_i)^2}{\sum (x_i - \overline{x}_i)^2} \tag{12}$$

2.7.3 Mean squared error

The mean squared error (MSE), also known as mean squared deviation (MSD), for an estimator (a method used to estimate an unobserved quantity) evaluates the average of the squared discrepancies, which is essentially the average of the squared differences between the estimated values and the true value. MSE serves as a risk function, representing the anticipated value of the squared error loss.

$$MSE = \frac{\sum (x_i - \widehat{x}_i)^2}{n} \tag{13}$$

2.7.4 Root mean square error

The root mean square error (RMSE) is a widely employed metric for assessing the precision of a statistical model or prediction algorithm. It quantifies the disparity between anticipated and observed values within a dataset [51]. To compute RMSE, one takes the square root of the average of the squared disparities between predicted and actual values. This metric is denominated in the same units as the data, providing an indication of the average magnitude of deviations between predicted and actual values. The formula for RMSE is as follows:

$$\boldsymbol{RMSE} = \sqrt{\frac{\sum (x_i - \widehat{x}_i)^2}{n}} \tag{14}$$

2.7.5 Mean absolute error

The mean absolute error (MAE) is a measurement used to determine the average discrepancy between predicted values and actual values within a dataset, without considering the direction of the errors. This is computed by finding the mean of the absolute differences between the predicted and actual values [52]. In mathematical terms, MAE can be expressed as:

$$MAE = \frac{1}{n}\sum |x_i - \widehat{x}_i| \tag{15}$$

For $i = 1, 2, 3 \dots .n$ Where $x_i, \widehat{x}_i, \overline{x}_i$, and n represent the original values, predicted values, the average value of the original data, and the total number of data instances, respectively.

3. Results and discussion

Table 1 demonstrates a high coefficient of determination (DC) ranging from 80 to 95%, which is highly commendable for a predictive model. The independent variables include RH, WS, Tmin, Tmax, and T. Analyzing the correlation matrix between SR and each input reveals a strong and positive correlation between SR and Tmin, Tmax, and T. Consequently, a model of SR incorporating these temperature variables, known as M1, has been developed. The statistical indicators (DC, RMSE, DC, MSE, and MAE) in **Table 1** outline the model's accuracy. The performance of individual models, namely ANFIS-GP, ANFIS-SC, and their combination (ensemble), has been thoroughly evaluated. During the evaluation process, 80% of the data is used for training, while the remaining 20% is reserved for testing. Various statistical metrics are employed to assess the models' performance, focusing on both the goodness of fit and performance error. The results are presented in **Table 1**, which clearly indicates that model M1 provides a significantly accurate prediction of solar radiation. Additionally, the ensemble method outperforms the individual models, with a DC of 95% compared to 80% for ANFIS-SC and 93% for ANFIS-GP.

The result highlights the efficacy of ensemble approaches in enhancing predictive accuracy and reaffirms their value in practical applications.

Training							
	Methods	**R**	**DC**	**MSE**	**RMSE**	**MAE**
M1	GP	0.964419	0.930103	0.030505	0.174656	0.119767
	SC	0.898913	0.808045	0.083774	0.289437	0.203251
	ENS	**0.97688**	**0.954294**	**0.019947**	**0.141235**	**0.101438**
Testing						
M1	GP	0.959621	0.920873	0.027558	0.166006	0.11559
	SC	0.863194	0.745104	0.088774	0.297949	0.211935
	ENS	**0.971104**	**0.943043**	**0.019837**	**0.140843**	**0.103832**

Table 1.
Performance evaluation of the models.

The provided results showcase the performance of the model using different optimization algorithms for training and testing. The three methods, ANFIS-GP, ANFIS-SC, and the ensemble (ENS), were evaluated based on key statistical metrics, such as correlation coefficient (R), determination coefficient (DC), mean squared error (MSE), root mean squared error (RMSE), and mean absolute error (MAE). It is evident from the training and testing results that the ensemble method (M1-ENS) consistently outperforms the individual ANFIS-SC (M1-SC) and ANFIS-GP (M1-GP) models in terms of R, DC, MSE, RMSE, and MAE. The ensemble approach showcases higher values for R and DC, indicating a stronger correlation and better determination capabilities. Additionally, it demonstrates lower values for MSE, RMSE, and MAE, which signify reduced prediction errors and enhanced accuracy.

To provide a clearer understanding of the predictive model's performance error, specifically in terms of RMSE, a bar chart can visually illustrate the comparative analysis. **Figure 5** displays the RMSE values for all training algorithms applied to model M1, demonstrating that they fall within the acceptable range during both the training and testing stages. This reaffirms the models' exceptional ability to effectively capture the complex relationship between the predictors and solar radiation (**Figure 6**).

From the graph above, it can be seen that ANFIS-ENS, having the least RMSE, outperformed both the individual models, ANFIS-GP and ANFIS-SC. The performance ranking of the models in M1 for both training and testing is as follows: ENS > GP > SC.

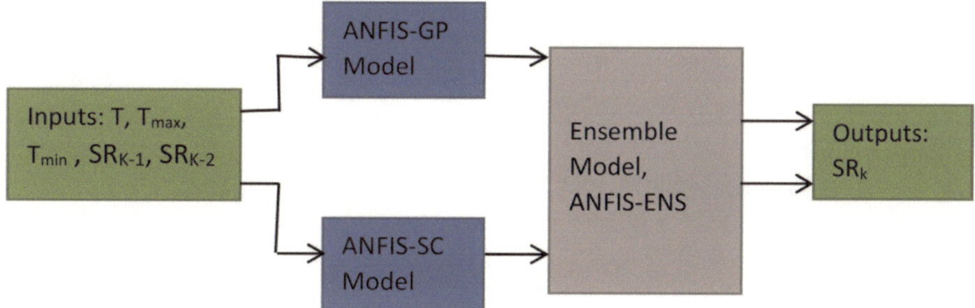

Figure 5.
Block diagram of the models.

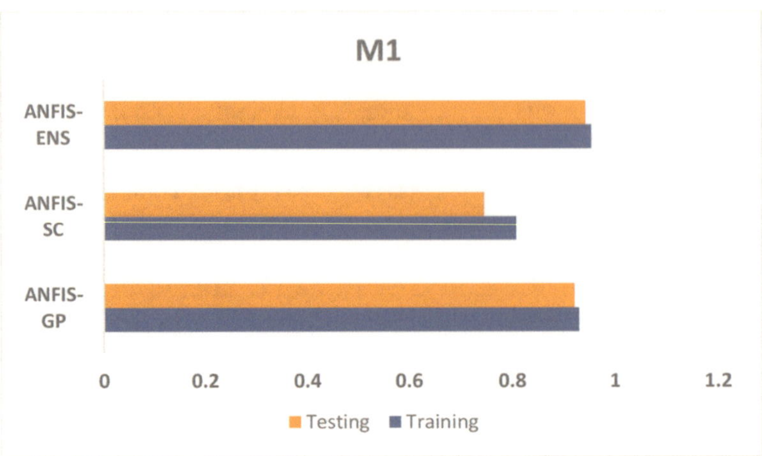

Figure 6.
Performance comparison of model M1.

The radar chart in **Figure 7** provides a clear view of the comparison of the models ANFIS-GP, ANFIS-SC, and ANFIS-ENS based on the coefficient of determination (DC). The models with their DC values closer to 1 generally have more accuracy. Hence, the order of accuracy of the three models developed can be ranked in terms of accuracy from highest to lowest as $ENS > GP > SC$.

In the present study, we developed an ANFIS Ensemble model to predict solar radiation in Kano State, Nigeria. The achieved accuracy of 0.9543 (DC values) demonstrates the effectiveness of our model. To discuss the results, let us compare them with the accuracies reported in the previous studies listed in the **Table 2** below.

Yohanna et al. [53] presented an empirical model for solar radiation prediction in Nigeria, achieving an accuracy of 0.608. This relatively low accuracy may be

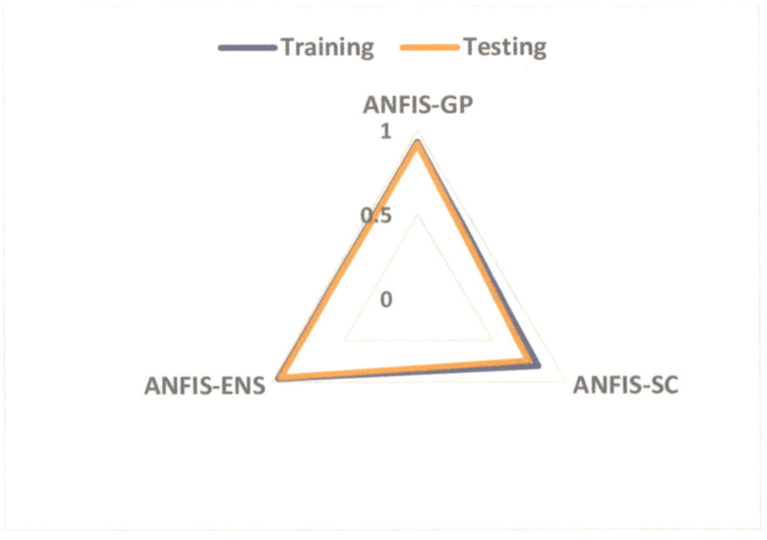

Figure 7.
Radar plot to compare the performance of the models.

Authors	Model type	Input parameters	Location	DC values
Yohanna et al. [53]	Empirical	3	Nigeria	0.608
Abdalla [54]	Empirical	4	Bahrain	0.780
Ramedani [55]	ANFIS	3	Iran	0.808
Olatomiwa et al. [56]	ANFIS	3	Nigeria	0.8544
Sajid and Ali [38]	ANFIS	3	Abu Dhabi	0.860
Sani S et al. [57]	ANFIS	4	Nigeria	0.8688
Present Study	ANFIS ENSEMBLE	3	Nigeria	0.9543

Table 2.
Comparison between the present study and the previous studies available from the literature.

attributed to the limitations of empirical models in capturing complex nonlinear relationships present in solar radiation data. Our ANFIS Ensemble model, with its ability to handle nonlinear relationships, significantly outperformed this empirical model.

Abdalla [54] also employed an empirical model, but in the context of Bahrain, achieving an accuracy of 0.780. Again, our ANFIS Ensemble model surpassed this accuracy, highlighting the advantages of using ANFIS techniques for solar radiation prediction.

Ramedani [55] utilized an ANFIS model in Iran and achieved an accuracy of 0.808. While our model demonstrates higher accuracy, it is essential to consider the differences in geographical locations and solar radiation patterns between Iran and Nigeria, which can influence prediction performance.

Olatomiwa et al. [56] developed an ANFIS model for solar radiation prediction in Nigeria, attaining an accuracy of 0.8544. Although their model performed well, our ANFIS Ensemble model surpassed it by a significant margin, illustrating the benefits of combining multiple ANFIS models.

Sajid and Ali [38] utilized an ANFIS model in Abu Dhabi, achieving an accuracy of 0.860. Again, our ANFIS Ensemble model outperformed their model, highlighting the effectiveness of our approach.

Sani S et al. [58] employed an ANFIS model with four input parameters for solar radiation prediction in Nigeria, attaining an accuracy of 0.8688. Our ANFIS Ensemble model exhibited a higher accuracy, showcasing the advantages of our ensemble approach even with a reduced number of input parameters.

In summary, our ANFIS Ensemble model achieved an accuracy of 0.9543, outperforming all the models compared in the **Table 2**. This indicates the superiority of our approach in accurately predicting solar radiation in Kano State, Nigeria. The ensemble technique, combining the strengths of individual ANFIS models, allowed us to achieve a more robust and accurate prediction. These results underscore the relevance and significance of our research, providing valuable insights into renewable energy systems, agricultural planning, and climate modeling in Kano State.

4. Conclusion

This study explored the application of ensemble machine-learning algorithms for predicting solar radiation in Kano, Nigeria. The primary objective was to develop robust machine-learning models for estimating solar radiation. Meteorological data consisting of four parameters, namely Maximum-Temperature (Tmax), Minimum-Temperature (Tmin), Mean-Temperature (Tmean), and solar radiation, were utilized. The data covered daily average values over a period of 12 months (January to December 2018). To enhance the predictive performance, the study employed an ensemble model by combining two optimization techniques: sub-clustering and grid-partitioning methods. The results were assessed using various evaluation metrics such as "R, DC, MSE, RMSE, and MAE" to ensure a comprehensive analysis and avoid bias, leading to better generalization of accuracy. The findings demonstrate that utilizing the ensemble approach yields more credible and acceptable outcomes. This research contributes to the development of reliable predictive models for solar radiation estimation, which can have significant implications in various applications and decision-making processes related to renewable energy utilization. Overall, the combination of ensemble machine learning and meteorological data proves to be a promising approach for accurate solar radiation prediction in the specific region of Kano, Nigeria.

Recommendations

The following will be recommended for future work:

i. Application of the ensemble approach on hourly solar radiation estimation instead of the daily averages.

ii. Other sophisticated machine learning methods such as hybrid machine learning, emotional neural network, and deep learning technique will be implemented with a larger dataset to have a more general view.

iii. Employ the Internet of Things technologies (IoT) along with smart sensors and sensor networks to achieve a real-time data collection and solar radiation estimation.

iv. The research will also consider more cities in Nigeria.

Acknowledgements

The authors would like to appreciate the effort of the Nigerian Meteorological Agency (NIMET) for providing the required data for this research.

Author details

Ammar Muhammad Ibrahim[1*], Salisu Muhammad Lawan[2], Rabiu Abdulkadir[3], Nazifi Sani Shuaibu[4], Muhammad Uzair[5], Musbahu Garba Indabawa[2], Masud Ibrahim[1] and Abdullahi Mahmoud Aliyu[2]

1 Department of Electrical Engineering, Binyaminu Usman Polytechnic, Hadejia, Jigawa State, Nigeria

2 Faculty of Engineering, Department of Electrical Engineering, Aliko Dangote University of Science and Technology, Kano, Nigeria

3 Faculty of Engineering, Department of Mechatronics Engineering, Aliko Dangote University of Science and Technology, Kano, Nigeria

4 College of Information Science and Electronic Engineering, Zhejiang University, Hangzhou, China

5 Faculty of Science, Department of Physics, Sule Lamido University, Kafin Hausa, Jigawa State, Nigeria

*Address all correspondence to: ammarmuhammad426@gmail.com

References

[1] Kosmadakis G, Karellas S, Kakaras E. Renewable and Conventional Electricity Generation Systems: Technologies and Diversity of Energy Systems. London: Springer; 2013. DOI: 10.1007/978-1-4471-5595-9

[2] Prakash R, Krishnan I. Energy , economics and environmental impacts of renewable energy systems energy, economics and environmental impacts of renewable energy systems. Renewable and Sustainable Energy Reviews. 2009;**13**: 2716-2721. DOI: 10.1016/j.rser.2009.05.007

[3] Panwar NL, Kaushik SC, Kothari S. Role of renewable energy sources in environmental protection: A review. Renewable and Sustainable Energy Reviews. 2011;**15**(3):1513-1524. DOI: 10.1016/j.rser.2010.11.037

[4] Dowell J, Pinson P. Very-Short-Term Probabilistic Wind Power Forecasts by Sparse Vector Autoregression. IEEE Transactions on Smart Grid. 2016;7:763-770. DOI: 10.1109/TSG.2015.2424078

[5] I. Renewable and E. Agency. Renewable Energy Statistics 2018 Statistiques D' Énergie Renouvelable 2018 Estadísticas De Energía. I. Renewable and E. Agency; 2018

[6] Reddy SS. Optimization of renewable energy resources in hybrid energy systems. 2017;7:43-60. DOI: 10.13052/jge1904-4720.7123

[7] Alkesaiberi AH, Fouzi Sun Y. Efficient Wind Power Prediction Using Machine Learning Methods: A Comparative Study. 2022;**15**. DOI: 10.3390/en15072327

[8] Jahani B. A Comparison between the Application of Empirical and ANN Methods for Estimation of Daily Global Solar Radiation in Iran; 2018;**13**. DOI: 10.1007/s12517-020-05437-0

[9] Yaniktepe B, Kara O, Ozalp C. Technoeconomic evaluation for an installed small-scale photovoltaic power plant. 2017;**2017**

[10] R. Energy. Renewable Energy Policies in a Time of Transition. ISBN: 9789292600617

[11] Ahmed R, Sreeram V, Mishra Y, Arif MD. A review and evaluation of the state-of-the-art in PV solar power forecasting: Techniques and optimization. Renewable and Sustainable Energy Reviews. 2020;**124**:109792. DOI: 10.1016/j.rser.2020.109792

[12] Dey BK, Khan I, Abhinav MN, Bhattacharjee A. Mathematical modelling and characteristic analysis of solar PV cell. In: 7th IEEE Annu. Inf. Technol. Electron. Mob. Commun. Conf. IEEE IEMCON 2016. 2016. DOI: 10.1109/IEMCON.2016.7746318

[13] Teke A, Ba H, Çelik Ö. Evaluation and performance comparison of different models for the estimation of solar radiation. 2015;**50**:1097-1107. DOI: 10.1016/j.rser.2015.05.049

[14] Almorox J, Hontoria C, Benito M. Models for obtaining daily global solar radiation with measured air temperature data in Madrid (Spain). Applied Energy. 2011;**88**(5):1703-1709. DOI: 10.1016/j.apenergy.2010.11.003

[15] Ali-Ou-Salah H, Oukarfi B, Bahani K, Moujabbir M. A new hybrid model for hourly solar radiation forecasting using daily classification technique and machine learning algorithms. Mathematical Problems in Engineering. 2021;**2021**. DOI: 10.1155/2021/6692626

[16] Akhter MN, Mekhilef S, Mokhlis H, Shah NM. Review on forecasting of photovoltaic power generation based on machine learning and metaheuristic techniques. IET Renewable Power Generation. 2019;**13**(7):1009-1023. DOI: 10.1049/iet-rpg.2018.5649

[17] Zhou Y, Liu Y, Wang D, Liu X, Wang Y. A review on global solar radiation prediction with machine learning models in a comprehensive perspective. Energy Conversion and Management. 2021;**235**(13):113960. DOI: 10.1016/j.enconman.2021.113960

[18] Fraihat H, Almbaideen AA, Al-Odienat A, Al-Naami B, De Fazio R, Visconti P. Solar radiation forecasting by Pearson correlation using LSTM neural network and ANFIS method: Application in the west-Central Jordan. Future Internet. 2022;**14**(3). DOI: 10.3390/fi14030079

[19] Chen W, Li DH, Li S, Lam JC. Estimating hourly global solar irradiance using artificial neural networks - a case study of Hong Kong. IOP Conference Series: Materials Science and Engineering. 2019;**556**(1):012043. DOI: 10.1088/1757-899X/556/1/012043

[20] Guermoui M, Rabehi A, Lalmi D. Multi-step ahead forecasting of daily solar radiation components in Saharan climate multi-step ahead forecasting of daily solar radiation components in Saharan climate. International Journal of Ambient Energy. 2018;**41**:1-23. DOI: 10.1080/01430750.2018.1490349

[21] Linares-rodríguez A, Ruiz-arias JA, Pozo-vázquez D, Tovar-pescador J. Generation of synthetic daily global solar radiation data based on ERA-interim reanalysis and arti fi cial neural networks. Energy. 2011;**36**(8):5356-5365. DOI: 10.1016/j.energy.2011.06.044

[22] Sözen A, Arcaklioglu E, Özalp M. Estimation of solar potential in Turkey by artificial neural networks using meteorological and geographical data. Energy Conversion and Management. 2004;**45**(18–19):3033-3052. DOI: 10.1016/j.enconman.2003.12.020

[23] Piri J, Kisi O. Modelling solar radiation reached to the earth using ANFIS, NN-ARX, and empirical models (case studies: Zahedan and Bojnurd stations). Journal of Atmospheric and Solar-Terrestrial Physics. 2015;**123**:39-47. DOI: 10.1016/j.jastp.2014.12.006

[24] Salcedo-Sanz S, Deo RC, Cornejo-Bueno L, Camacho-Gómez C, Ghimire S. An efficient neuro-evolutionary hybrid modelling mechanism for the estimation of daily global solar radiation in the sunshine state of Australia. Applied Energy. 2018;**209**:79-94. DOI: 10.1016/j.apenergy.2017.10.076

[25] Mohammadi K, Shamshirband S, Hossein M, Amjad K, Petkovic D. Support vector regression based prediction of global solar radiation on a horizontal surface. 2015;**91**:433-441. DOI: 10.1016/j.enconman.2014.12.015

[26] Naderloo L. Prediction of solar radiation on the horizon using neural network methods, ANFIS and RSM (case study: Sarpol-e-Zahab township, Iran). Journal of Earth System Science. 2020;**129**(1). DOI: 10.1007/s12040-020-01414-z

[27] Wang L et al. Prediction of solar radiation in China using different adaptive neuro-fuzzy methods and M5 model tree. International Journal of Climatology. 2017;**37**(3):1141-1155. DOI: 10.1002/joc.4762

[28] Cobos FF et al. Assessment of the impact of meteorological conditions on pyrheliometer calibration. Solar Energy.

2018;**168**:44-59. DOI: 10.1016/j.solener. 2018.03.046

[29] Yildirim A, Bilgili M, Ozbek A. One-hour-ahead solar radiation forecasting by MLP, LSTM, and ANFIS approaches. Meteorology and Atmospheric Physics. 2023;**135**(1):1-17. DOI: 10.1007/ s00703-022-00946-x

[30] Tao H et al. Global solar radiation prediction over North Dakota using air temperature: Development of novel hybrid intelligence model. Energy Reports. 2021;**7**:136-157. DOI: 10.1016/j. egyr.2020.11.033

[31] Abba SI, Pham QB, Saini G, Thi N, Linh T, and Ahmed AN. Implementation of Data Intelligence Models Coupled with Ensemble Machine Learning for Prediction of Water Quality Index; 2020

[32] Selin AGU, Abba ISI. A novel multi - model data - driven ensemble technique for the prediction of retention factor in HPLC method development. Chromatographia. 2020;**83**:933-945. DOI: 10.1007/s10337-020-03912-0

[33] Ammar MI et al. Improving the prediction of solar radiation using ANFIS optimization ensemble; **1**(5):1-13. DOI: 10.1007/978-3-320-59427-9

[34] Sciences H, Journal J, August H. Comparative implementation between neuro-emotional genetic algorithm and novel ensemble computing techniques for modelling dissolved oxygen comparative implementation between neuro- emotional genetic algorithm and novel ensemble computing techniques for m. Hydrological Sciences Journal. 2021;**66**(10):1-13. DOI: 10.1080/ 02626667.2021.1937179

[35] Jang JR. ANFIS: Adap Tive-Ne Twork-Based Fuzzy Inference System. Vol. 23 (3)1993

[36] Salisu S, Mustafa MW, Mustapha M. Predicting Global Solar Radiation in Nigeria Using Adaptive Neuro-Fuzzy Approach. Vol. 2. Cham: Springer; 2018. DOI: 10.1007/978-3-319-59427-9

[37] Abdulkadir RA, Wudil T, Gaya MS, Shauket S, Muhammad UG. Effluents quality prediction by using nonlinear dynamic block-oriented models : A system identification approach effluents quality prediction by using nonlinear dynamic block-oriented models: A system identification approach. 2021;**218**:52-62. DOI: 10.5004/dwt.2021.26983

[38] Hussain S, Al Alili A. Soft computing approach for solar radiation prediction over Abu Dhabi, UAE: A comparative analysis. In: International Conference on Smart Energy Grid Engineering SEGE. Vol. 2015. 2015. pp. 1-6. DOI: 10.1109/ SEGE.2015.7324613

[39] Rathnayake N, Dang TL, Hoshino Y. A novel optimization algorithm: Cascaded adaptive neuro-fuzzy inference system. International Journal of Fuzzy Systems. 2021;**23**(7):1955-1971. DOI: 10.1007/s40815-021-01076-z

[40] Maroufpoor S, Shauket S, Al-ansari N, Malik A. A novel hybridized neuro-fuzzy model with an optimal input combination for dissolved oxygen estimation. 2022;**10**:929707

[41] Zubaidi SL et al. A novel methodology for prediction urban water demand by wavelet denoising and adaptive neuro-fuzzy inference system approach. Water (Switzerland). 2020;**12** (6). DOI: 10.3390/w12061628

[42] Yavarian K, Mohammadian A, Hashemi F. Adaptive neuro fuzzy inference system PID controller for AVR system using SNR-PSO optimization adaptive neuro fuzzy inference system PID controller for AVR system using

SNR-PSO optimization. International Journal on Electrical Engineering and Informatics. 2016;**7**:394-408. DOI: 10.15676/ijeei.2015.7.3.3

[43] Yaseen ZM, Ramal MM. Hybrid Adaptive Neuro-Fuzzy Models for Water Quality Index Estimation; 2018

[44] Choubin B, Darabi H, Rahmati O, Sajedi-hosseini F, Kløve B. Science of the Total Environment River suspended sediment modelling using the CART model: A comparative study of machine learning techniques. Science of the Total Environment. 2018;**615**:272-281. DOI: 10.1016/j.scitotenv.2017.09.293

[45] Taylor P, Bezdek JC. Cluster validity with fuzzy sets. Journal of Cybernetics. 2008;**3**:37-41. DOI: 10.1080/0196972730 8546047

[46] Halkidi M, Batistakis Y, Vazirgiannis M. Cluster validity methods: Part I. 2002;**31**(2):40-45

[47] Arbelaitz O, Gurrutxaga I, Muguerza J. An extensive comparative study of cluster validity indices. 2013;**46**: 243-256. DOI: 10.1016/j. patcog.2012.07.021

[48] Zang H, Liu L, Sun L, Cheng L, Wei Z, Sun G. Short-term global horizontal irradiance forecasting based on a hybrid CNN-LSTM model with spatiotemporal correlations. Renewable Energy. 2020;**160**:26-41. DOI: 10.1016/ j.renene.2020.05.150

[49] Antor AF, Wollega ED. Comparison of machine learning algorithms for wind speed prediction. In: Proceedings of the 5th NA International Conference on Industrial Engineering and Operations Management Detroit, Michigan, USA, August 10 - 14, 2020. 2020. pp. 857-866

[50] He C et al. Improving solar radiation estimation in China based on regional optimal combination of meteorological factors with machine learning methods. Energy Conversion and Management. 2020;**220**:113111. DOI: 10.1016/j. enconman.2020.113111

[51] Lawan SM, Abidin WAWZ, Chai WY, Baharun A, Masri T. Different models of wind speed prediction: A comprehensive review. 2014;**5**(1)

[52] Dalianis H. Evaluation metrics and evaluation. Clinical Text Mining. 2018; **1967**:45-53. DOI: 10.1007/978-3-319-78503-5_6

[53] Yohanna JK, Itodo IN, Umogbai VI. A model for determining the global solar radiation for Makurdi, Nigeria. Renewable Energy. 2011;**36**(7):1989-1992. DOI: 10.1016/j.renene.2010.12.028

[54] Taylor P, Abdalla YAG. New correlations of global solar radiation with meteorological parameters for Bahrain new correlations of global solar radiation with meteorological. International Journal of Solar Energy. 2007;**2013**:37-41

[55] Ramedani Z, Omid M, Keyhani A, Shamshirband S, Khoshnevisan B. Potential of radial basis function based support vector regression for global solar radiation prediction. Renewable and Sustainable Energy Reviews. 2014;**39**: 1005-1011. DOI: 10.1016/j.rser.2014. 07.108

[56] Olatomiwa L, Mekhilef S, Shamshirband S, Petković D. Adaptive neuro-fuzzy approach for solar radiation prediction in Nigeria. Renewable and Sustainable Energy Reviews. 2015;**51**: 1784-1791. DOI: 10.1016/j.rser.2015. 05.068

[57] Salisu S, Mustafa MW, Mustapha M. Predicting global solar radiation in Nigeria using adaptive neuro-fuzzy approach. Lecture Notes on Data

Engineering and Communications Technologies. 2018;**5**:513-521. DOI: 10.1007/978-3-319-59427-9_54

[58] Gaya MS, Wahab NA, Sam Y, Samsuddin SI. Comparison of ANFIS and neural network direct inverse control applied to wastewater treatment system. 2014;**845**:543-548. DOI: 10.4028/www.scientific.net/AMR.845.543

Chapter 4

Application of Adaptive Neuro-Fuzzy Inference System Control in Power Systems

Ginarsa I. Made, Nrartha I. Made Ari, Muljono Agung Budi and Ardana I. Putu

Abstract

An adaptive neuro-fuzzy inference system (ANFIS) is developed by combining neural-networks and fuzzy system. The ANFIS model uses the advantages possessed by the properties of neural networks and its decision making is based on fuzzy inference. The ANFIS parameters are obtained and updated by training processes. The ANFIS consists of two inputs (by Gaussian or other membership function) and an output (with constant or linear membership function). The ANFIS control is implemented by building a power system stabilizer (PSS) in power systems. The PSS function is to produce an additional stabilizing signal on the reactive mode of the generator. Training data are obtained from the systems that controlled by a conventional PSS with various conditions. The training process is carried out repeatedly until the appropriate ANFIS parameters are found. Next, the PSS based on ANFIS is applied to replace the conventional PSS on a single machine and hybrid power plants. Peak overshoot and settling time of the power systems are smaller and shorter. The ANFIS PSS makes the power system stability improve significantly in small-signal studies.

Keywords: ANFIS, control, hybrid plant, stability improvement, power systems

1. Introduction

Artificial intelligence (AI) includes an adaptive neuro-fuzzy inference system (ANFIS) intensively developed in recent years. So, the application of the ANFIS model penetrates some research fields. Especially in electrical engineering, some researchers implement this model on solar-cell generation to enhance performance [1], on a combination of photovoltaic and grid systems to maximize profit [2], on power management under variations of climate conditions [3], on islanding detection for low voltage micro-grid power system [4], and to reduce the harmonic in solar cell connected to distribution systems [5]. Recognizing data patterns from multiple inputs and mapping them into output precisely is the ability of the ANFIS algorithm. This ability is acquired through training sessions. During the training session, the parameters of the ANFIS are modified and updated based on training data using hybrid Aquila arithmetic [5] and artificial bee colony optimization techniques [6]. The ANFIS

IntechOpen

model is applied on control renewable energy system [7] and estimator collaborated with intelligent passivity control is used to regulate the grid-tied inverter in various operating conditions [8]. Forecasting power production in solar cell is done using the ANFIS combined with genetic algorithm [9]. The ANFIS improvement proposed to evaluate the partial discharge intensity on electrical equipment. This methods is used to search the electric insulation defects, especially for high voltage or ultra-high voltage applications [10] and to design the optimal based on the size, shape, and panel of active tower transmission system combine by biogeography-based optimization (BBO) algorithm [11]. Also, the ANFIS algorithm was applied to mitigate the frequency deviation on automatic generation control (AGC) [12] and load frequency control (LFC) [13] in multi area power systems, to minimize the error on load forecast [14], and to classify the faults type and location of a power transformer [15]. The virtual inductance tuned based on ANFIS model is used to improve small-signal stability and to control reactive power sharing in micro-grid power system [16]. The ANFIS model is used to control the fluctuation of the blade pitch in wind power plant [17]. The ANFIS is applied to control chaos and voltage collapse in power systems [18, 19], transient improvement in power systems [20] and in high voltage direct current (HVDC) transmission system [21].

2. Adaptive neuro-fuzzy inference system (ANFIS) theory

The ANFIS model bridges how to use the advantage properties of artificial neural networks (ANN) that can process data in parallel mode, recognize pattern, learn and practice in solving a problem without mathematical modeling, and build a model by using some data sets. Parameters of the ANN are adjusted and updated by training process. Furthermore, Takagi-Sugeno Tsukamoto (TSK) fuzzy inference scheme carried out to make a decision or inference. The ANFIS model consists of 5 layers, and general structure the ANFIS model shown in **Figure 1**. **Figure 1** describes two crisp inputs (In1 and In2) and one crisp output (f). Fixed and adaptive node functions are represented by circles and squares, respectively. Membership function (MF), weight and rules locate in hidden layer. The data sets should be uniform and free from unrecognized data are used to train the ANFIS model. The MF parameters are

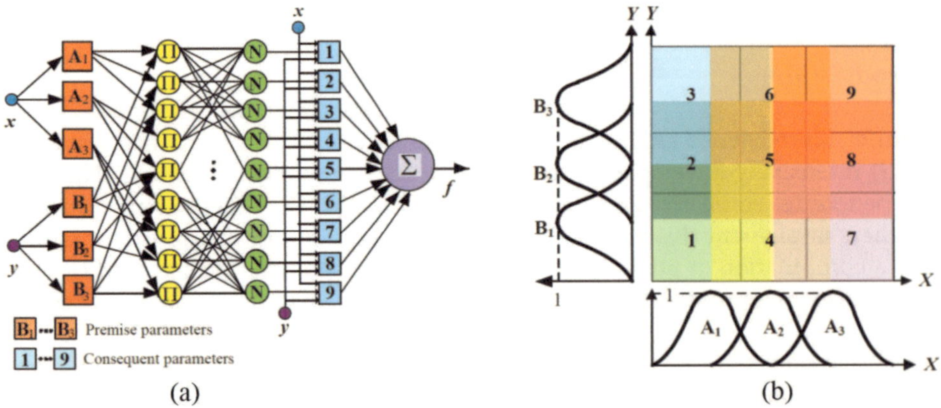

Figure 1.
Illustration of the ANFIS model. (a). Structure of ANFIS 2 inputs and 1 output (b). Rules matrix from input-output MF.

obtained automatically through training sessions using back-propagation and least squared estimation (LSE) methods. This training process conducted until the root mean squared error (RMSE) is small enough (Exp. LSE = 10^{-5}). The ANFIS allows only the Sugeno-type FIS. **Figure 2** illustrates architecture of the ANFIS comprises antecedent and conclusions as component majority. To simplify the input–output index for networks, we use it for mapping inputs (i, j = 1,2,3) and ($f_{ij} = f_{11}, \dots, f_{33} = f_k = f_1, \dots, f_9$).

$$\text{Rule } k: \text{If } x \text{ is } A_i \text{ and } y \text{ is } B_j; \text{then } f_k = p_k x + q_k y + r_k \tag{1}$$

$$\text{Rule } 1: \text{If } x \text{ is } A_1 \text{ and } y \text{ is } B_1; \text{then } f_1 = p_1 x + q_1 y + r_1.$$

$$\text{Rule } 2: \text{If } x \text{ is } A_2 \text{ and } y \text{ is } B_1; \text{then } f_2 = p_2 x + q_2 y + r_2$$

$$\vdots$$

$$\text{Rule } 9: \text{If } x \text{ is } A_3 \text{ and } y \text{ is } B_3; \text{then } f_9 = p_9 x + q_9 y + r_9$$

Ly1: Node in this layer is an adaptive node and the function is

$$\begin{array}{c} K_{1,i} = \mu_{A_i}(x), i = 1, 2, 3, \text{or} \\ K_{1,j} = \mu_{B_j}(y), j = 1, 2, 3 \end{array} \tag{2}$$

Where x and y are the inputs to node i, and Ai and Bi are linguistic labels (such as low, medium, or high) concerning this node. The $K_{1,i}$ is the membership grade of a fuzzy set A, in this case (A1, A2, ..., B3), and it is used to determine the membership grade of input A. The Gauss-type membership function for A is used in this topic and formulated as:

$$g(x; c, \sigma) = e^{-\frac{1}{2}\left(\frac{x-c}{\sigma}\right)^2} \tag{3}$$

A Gauss MF is represented by two parameters c and σ. Where c and σ are the center and width of the Gauss MF, respectively.

Ly2: Node in this layer (Ly2) is a fixed node. The node and is labeled by operator (symbol) Π. The function products all of incoming signals and performs fuzzy operator AND. The output formula is as follows:

$$K_{2,k} = w_{ij} = \mu_{A_i}(x) \times \mu_{B_j}(y); i, j = 1, 2, 3; k = 1, 2, \dots, 9 \tag{4}$$

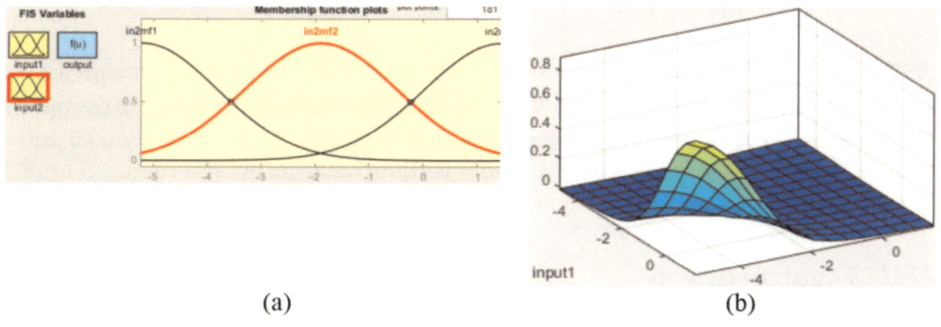

Figure 2.
The ANFIS model is formed after the training stage. (a) Three Gaussian MF on Input 2 (b) Surface control of input-output.

Ly3: Every node in the layer Ly3 is a fixed node type and is given a label N. Ratio of the i-th rule's firing strengths to the sum of all rule's firing strengths are calculated in this node. Outputs of the layer Ly3 are namely normalized firing strengths, and the mathematical function written as:

$$K_{3,k} = \overline{w_{ij}} = \frac{W_{ij}}{W_{11} + W_{12} + \ldots + W_{33}} = \frac{W_{ij}}{\sum_{i,j=1}^{3} W_{ij}}, i,j = 1,2,3; k = 1,2,\ldots,9 \quad (5)$$

Ly4: The node in this layer (Ly4) is an adaptive node and the function is expressed as follow:

$$K_{4,k} = \overline{w_{ij}} f_k = \overline{w_{ij}}\left(p_k x + q_k y + r_k\right), i,j = 1,2,3; k = 1,2,\ldots,9 \quad (6)$$

Where $\overline{w_{ij}}$ and (pk, qk and rk) are the normalized firing strength of Ly3 and parameters of this layer. The parameters in the layer Ly3 are referred as consequent parameters.

Ly5: Node in the layer Ly5 is a fixed node. This node is labeled by mathematical operator sigma (Σ). The overall outputs are the summation of all incoming signals computed in this node, and the function of this node is formulated as:

$$K_{5,1} = K_{5,k=1} = \sum_{i,j=1}^{3} \overline{w_{ij}} f_k = \frac{\sum_{i,j=1}^{3} w_{ij} f_k}{\sum_{i,j=1}^{3} w_{ij}}, i,j = 1,2,3; k = 1,2,\ldots,9 \quad (7)$$

Multi-layer feed-forward networks are formulated by mathematical expression as follows:

$$W_i = \mu_{Pi}(x) \times \mu_{Qi}(y); W_i = \frac{W_i}{W_1 + W_2}; i = 1,2 \quad (8)$$

$$W_i = \mu_{Pi}(x) \times \mu_{Qi}(y); W_i = \frac{W_i}{W_1 + W_2}; i = 1,2 \quad (9)$$

The membership function (MF) lies between value of 0 and 1, and it is evaluated using mathematical expression as follows:

$$\mu_{Pi}(x) = \frac{1}{1 + \left[\left((x - r_i)p_i^{-1}\right)^2\right]^{p_i - 3}}; \mu_{Pi}(x) = exp\left[-\left[\left(\frac{x - r_i}{p_i}\right)^2\right]^{b_i}\right] \quad (10)$$

Where p_i, r_i and b_i are parameters of the membership function. Input signal that in crisp value form is transformed into fuzzy value by considering the MF. Arrangement of MF shape and fuzzy inference system (FIS) settings are carried out by trial and error method in off-line mode until a model is found that meets the requirements.

3. ANFIS control design

The ANFIS algorithm in this scheme is used as a power system stabilizer (PSS) in a single machine model power system. The PSS function is to generate a stability signal which is modulated in the excitation system to improve power system stability.

Suppose we have a single-machine power system that supplies the infinite bus, the diagram model is simplified and illustrated in **Figure 3a**. The model and parameter data are taken from [22]. The first time is to collect the data input-output for training the ANFIS model that consist of 2 inputs (rotor speed deviation (om11) and its derivative (de11)), and one output (additional stability signal, vs). The data training is collected by running the system equipped with conventional PSS in variation mode, as shown in **Figure 3b**. The data training is obtained in 56 data points, so this data is formed into data training format using MATLAB in matrix form with 3 × 56. Then, the training data matrix is exported to the MATLAB workspace. Next, train the ANFIS model by running MATLAB's 'anfisedit' function. The training processes are done in off-line mode.

Figure 4a shows that the process to import the training, testing, and checking data points from the workspace in the anfisedit tool. Also, the iteration of the training process is in 30 Epochs. **Figure 4b** illustrates the choice of linguistic variables: There are three linguistic variables are applied to describe each input variable (Negative, NE; Zero, ZE; and Positive, PO. Gaussian membership functions (MFs) are implemented to represent the degree of membership variable inputs. The Gaussian MF is developed by two parameters (c and σ). The c and σ parameters are defined as the center and width of the MF, respectively. First-order Takagi-Sugeno fuzzy model is chosen for simplification of its model and to gain computational efficiency. The grid partition

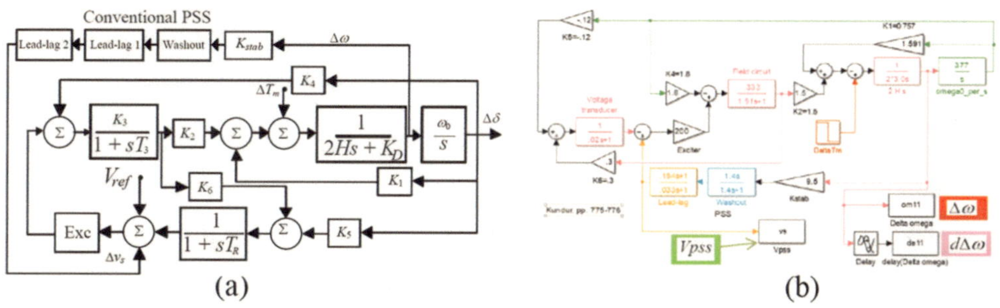

Figure 3.
Single machine for small signal stability model, (a) power system and PSS diagram block, (b), collecting data input-output for training ANFIS PSS.

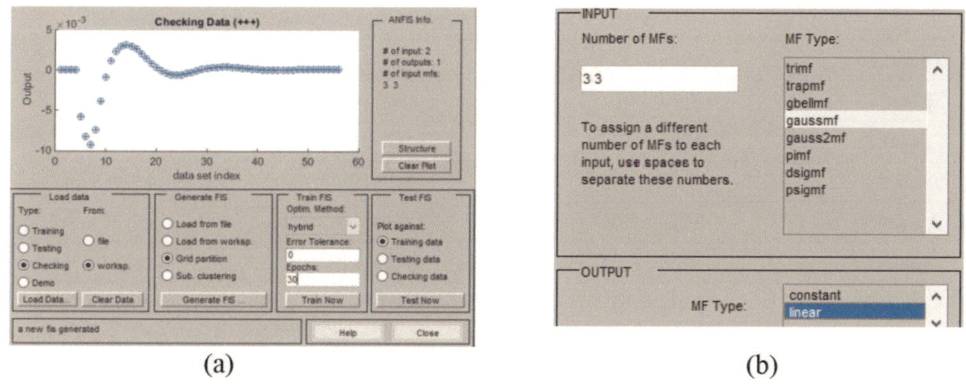

Figure 4.
The 'anfisedit' menu to input training data and set ANFIS parameters. (a) Import the train data from workspace (b). Input-output MF parameters.

method is applied to generate fuzzy inference system (FIS). The unknown parameters of the Gaussian MF such as width, center, and linear outputs of each rule are optimized using training data sets. All parameter's initial values are set to zero. The optimization method used to obtain parameters is hybrid or back-propagation and least squares estimation (LSE) method(s).

The ANFIS model formed in a few seconds during the training process. After some training stages pass, the result (ANFIS model) saves on the file with *.fis format in the MATLAB environment. The ANFIS model is ready to be embedded in the Simulink model to replace the conventional PSS in power system stability or other control system fields. This training session produces three Gaussian MFs for the Input 2 (a derivative of rotor speed deviation). This Gaussian MF illustration is depicted in **Figure 2a**. This training also generates an input-output mapping, where this mapping describes the relationship between the magnitude of the two input signals, and the signal magnitude generated in the control scheme. This mapping is applied to meet the output control signal, and the plant needs the control signal to improve the plant's or system's stability. The input-output surface control for this power system stabilizer is depicted in **Figure 2b** (**Tables 1** and **2**).

MF name	Parameter	
Input 1	σ (width) × 10^{-4}	c (center) × 10^{-4}
Δωmf1	1.309	−4.801
Δωmf2		−1.719
Δωmf3		1.363
Input 2		
dΔωmf1	1.411	−5.219
dΔωmf2		−1.895
dΔωmf3		1.429

Table 1.
Input variables: Type Gaussian; range: [−4.801 1.01] × 10^{-4}.

MF name	Parameter		
	p	q	R
Vpssmf1	5.996×10^{-2}	-6.46×10^{-4}	-5.878×10^{-3}
Vpssmf 2	-2.401×10^{-2}	-2.582×10^{-2}	-1.577×10^{-2}
Vpssmf 3	3.061×10^{-3}	3.562×10^{-3}	1.39×10^{-2}
Vpssmf 4	-2.202×10^{-2}	-2.55×10^{-2}	1.231×10^{-2}
Vpssmf 5	8.228×10^{-2}	7.295×10^{-2}	-5.722×10^{-3}
Vpssmf 6	-8.117×10^{-2}	-2.424×10^{-2}	-9.984×10^{-3}
Vpssmf 7	3.911×10^{-3}	-3.561×10^{-4}	1.013
Vpssmf 8	-1.716×10^{-2}	-2.909×10^{-2}	1.061×10^{-2}
Vpssmf 9	1.25×10^{-1}	-6.073×10^{-2}	-1.685×10^{-3}

Table 2.
Output variable: Type linear (orde 1); range: [−9.231 3.17] × 10^{-3}.

DOI: http://dx.doi.org/10.5772/intechopen.1004104

4. ANFIS control application

4.1 ANFIS-PSS for stability improvement in a single machine

The examination of ANFIS PSS was done by adding the load disturbing on the mechanical mode of power system. **Figure 5** shows the response on rotor speed deviation ($\Delta\omega$) of the power system for additional loading at 0.04 pu (4%). The single machine response for rotor speed deviation with additional loading (disturbance) at 0.02 and 0.04 pu (2 and 4%) is listed in **Table 3**. This response is used to assess the stability of the single machine. In this scenario, the machine was run without PSS, with conventional PSS, and with ANFIS-based PSS. From **Table 3** and **Figure 5**, the system response without PSS for peak overshoot (Mp) was obtained at -5.69×10^{-4} rad/s. Moreover, the system response without PSS was un-damped and oscillated, and the settling time (t_{st}) was more than 2 seconds (s). Meanwhile, the responses of the conventional and ANFIS PSS(s) for the peak overshoots were achieved at -3.84×10^{-4} and -3.69×10^{-4} rad/s, respectively. The settling times were obtained at the time 1.56 and .98 s the conventional and ANFIS PSS(s), respectively. From this scenario, the ANFIS PSS is more effective in improving the stability

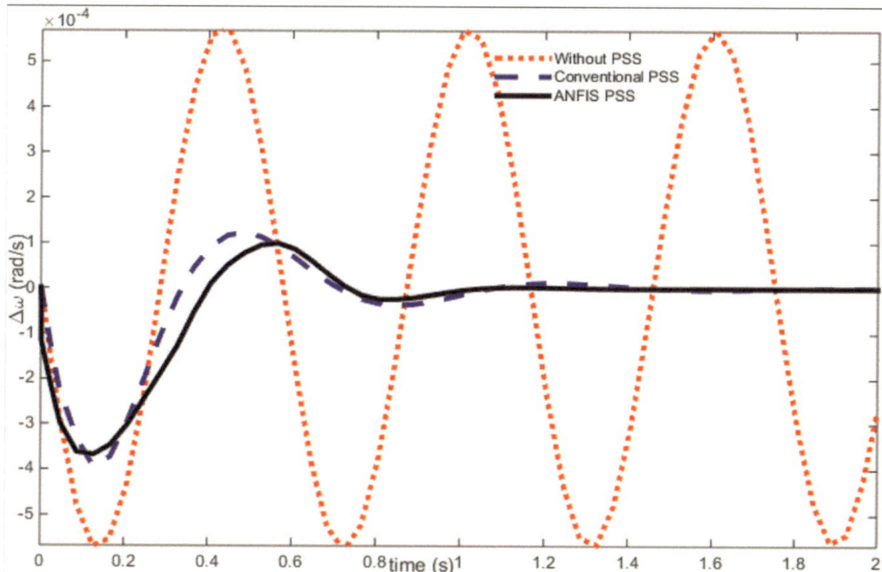

Figure 5.
Improvement of rotor speed deviation using ANFIS PSS.

Additional load disturbing (%)	Without PSS		Conventional PSS		ANFIS PSS	
	$M_p \times (-10^{-4})$ (rad/s)	t_{st} (s)	$M_p \times (-10^{-4})$ (rad/s)	t_{st} (s)	$M_p \times (-10^{-4})$ (rad/s)	t_{st} (s)
2	2.85	>2	1.92	1.62	1.72	.96
4	5.69		3.84	1.56	3.69	.98

Table 3.
Peak overshoot and settling time for rotor speed deviation.

of the single machine power system with less peak overshoot and shorter settling time for rotor speed deviation, compared to the other PSS.

The next session is explained the response for rotor angle (Δδ) and the simulation results are shown in **Figure 6** and **Table 4**, respectively. The peak overshoot was achieved at the values of −1.13, −.68, and − .66° for the system without the PSS, conventional PSS, and ANFIS PSS, for a disturbance at 2%. The settling time was achieved at times 1.61 and .95 s for the conventional PSS and ANFIS PSS. The rotor angle steady state was obtained at −.54 and − .57° for the system with the conventional PSS and ANFIS PSS, respectively.

Figure 6 shows the rotor angle response. The peak overshoot was obtained at 2.26° for disturbance 4%, and the single machine was not equipped by the PSS. The settling time of the response was more than 2 s. It monitored that the rotor angle response is un-damped and oscillated, and this condition is unwanted in stability studies. In the single machine equipped with the conventional PSS and ANFIS PSS, the simulation results are as follows. The peak overshoot of rotor angle was obtained at the values −1.54 and − 1.44° for the conventional PSS and ANFIS PSS, respectively. The responses of the rotor angle settled rapidly, and the settling value achieved around value 1.1°.

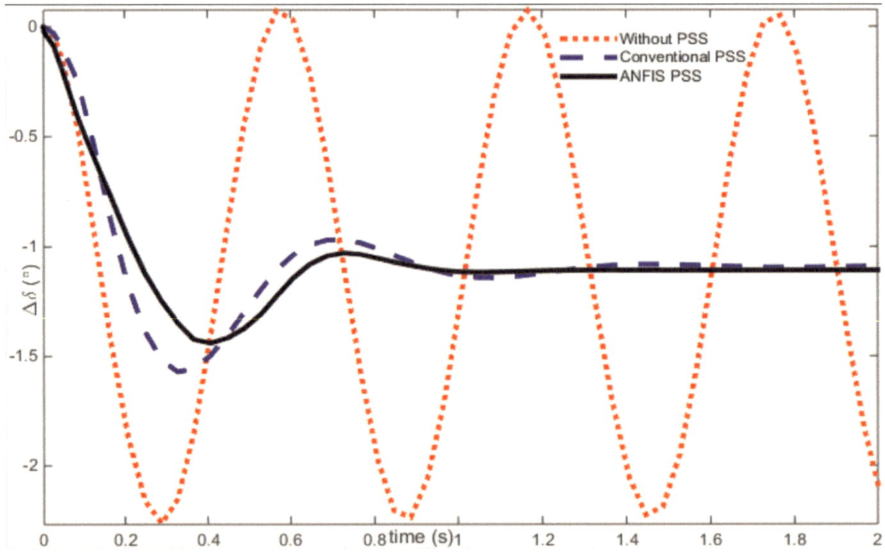

Figure 6.
Enhancement of rotor angle stability for disturbance 4%.

Additional load disturbing (%)	Without PSS			Conventional PSS			ANFIS PSS		
	$M_p \times -1$ (°)	t_{st} (s)	$\delta \times -1$ (°)	$M_p \times -1$ (°)	t_{st} (s)	$\delta \times -1$ (°)	$M_p \times -1$ (°)	t_{st} (s)	$\delta \times -1$ (°)
2	1.13	>2	osc	.68	1.61	.54	.66	.95	.57
4	2.26			1.54	1.63	1.095	1.44	.96	1.1

Table 4.
Peak overshoot and settling time for rotor angle.

4.2 ANFIS-PSS for stability maintain in hybrid power system

In this session, the Lombok Island Power Plant [23, 24] with a simplified model [25] is taken as an example of ANFIS power system stabilizer (PSS). The one-line diagram of the hybrid power system for small signal stability is depicted in **Figure 7**. The system consists of diesel power plant (DPP) and local load (L1) in Bus 1. Bus 4: Micro hydro power plant (MHPP) and load (L4). The two transformers (Tr1 and Tr4) connected from Bus 1 to Bus 5 and from Bus 4 to Bus 5, respectively. The transmission line (TL) connects the Bus 5 and Infinite bus. The PSS is installed at Generator 1 (G1) to improve stability of the whole system.

The system is equipped with a conventional PSS and simulated in varied PSS parameters and load disturbing in the Generator 1 (Machine 1) to get the ANFIS model. Several data training sets were collected from this simulation. The data training sets were used to train the ANFIS PSS model. The procedure for learning the ANFIS algorithm is similar to Section 3. The result of training stage is explained as follows: The ANFIS PSS model with two inputs (omega and d_omega) and one output (Vpss) is illustrated by some diagram blocks. This model is described in **Figure 8a**. The inputs omega and d_omega are the rotor speed deviation of Generator 1 and its derivative, respectively. The ANFIS-based PSS output is the additional stabilizer signal. This signal is fed to the excitation system Generator 1. The membership function (MF) for d_omega input is shown in **Figure 8b**, where the MFs consist of 5 type-2 Gauss MFs. The 25-linguistic-rule is used to illustrate the connection of the input and output parameters in the ANFIS PSS. This rule-based is depicted in **Figure 8c**. Also, the input-output mapping can be implemented by input-output surface control as shown in **Figure 8d**.

The system was disturbed by additional electrical power at 2 and 4% in Machine 1 to examine the performance of the ANFIS PSS, and the responses of respective PSS are shown **Figures 9–12**. The complete performances also are listed in **Tables 5–8**. **Figure 9** shows the improvement of rotor speed deviation for the Machine 1 disturbed by 4% at the Machine 1. The response for respective PSS is compared to prove the effectiveness of the ANFIS PSS over others in this graphic.

Table 5 lists the peak overshoot for disturbing 2% was achieved at −5.87, −4.43 and -3.38×10^{-4} rad/s, for the system without PSS, with the conventional PSS and ANFIS PSS, respectively. The settling time occurred at 1.81 and 1.42 s for the conventional PSS and ANFIS PSS. Moreover, the peak overshoot was obtained at −11.76,

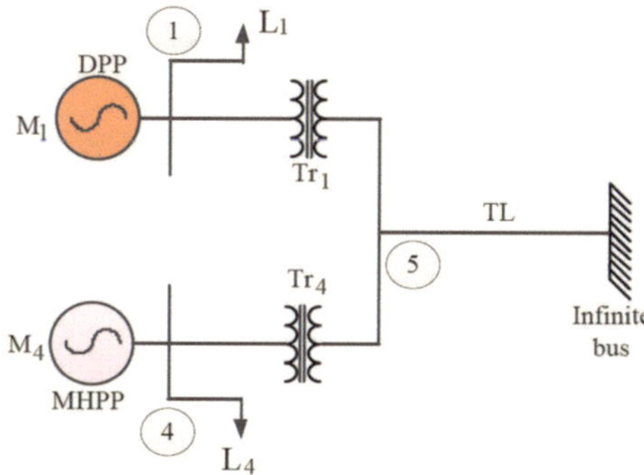

Figure 7.
The hybrid power system for small signal stability model.

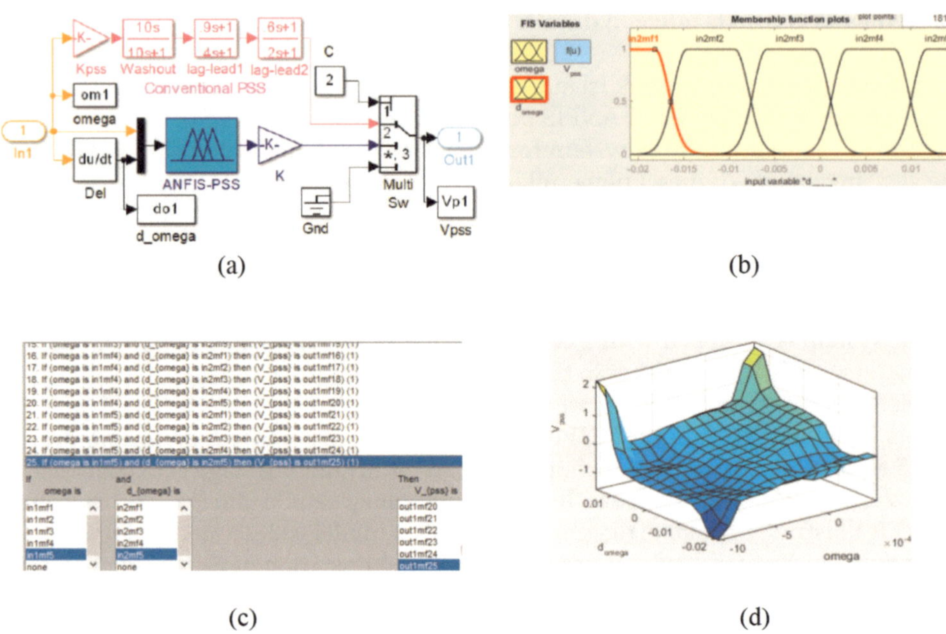

Figure 8.
ANFIS PSS for hybrid power plant. (a) ANFIS PSS in Simulink model (b) Gauss-2 type MF for d_omega input (c). A 25-ANFIS-rule for PSS Generator 1 (d) Surface control for ANFIS PSS.

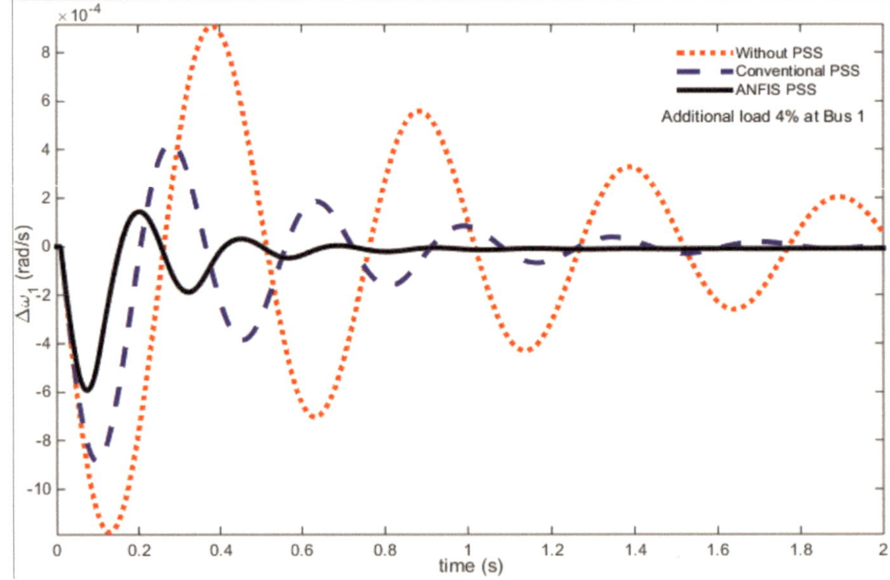

Figure 9.
Improvement of rotor speed deviation stability using ANFIS PSS.

-8.85 and -5.91×10^{-4} rad/s, for disturbance 4%. The system is settled at time 1.98 and 1.47 s, respectively, for the conventional PSS and ANFIS PSS.

The stability enhancement for rotor angle with the electrical load disturbing 4% is described in **Figure 10**. The rotor angle felt with first swing and the peak overshoot

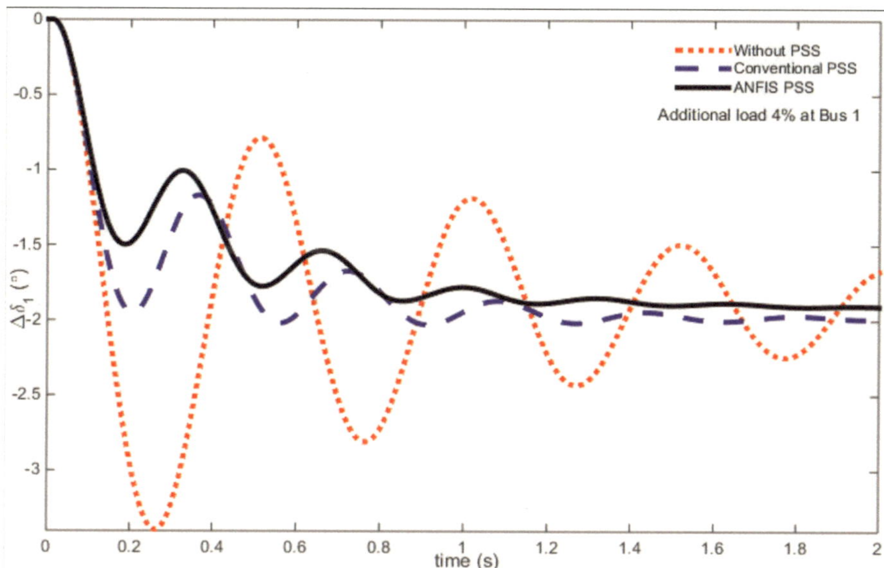

Figure 10.
Improvement of rotor angle stability using ANFIS PSS.

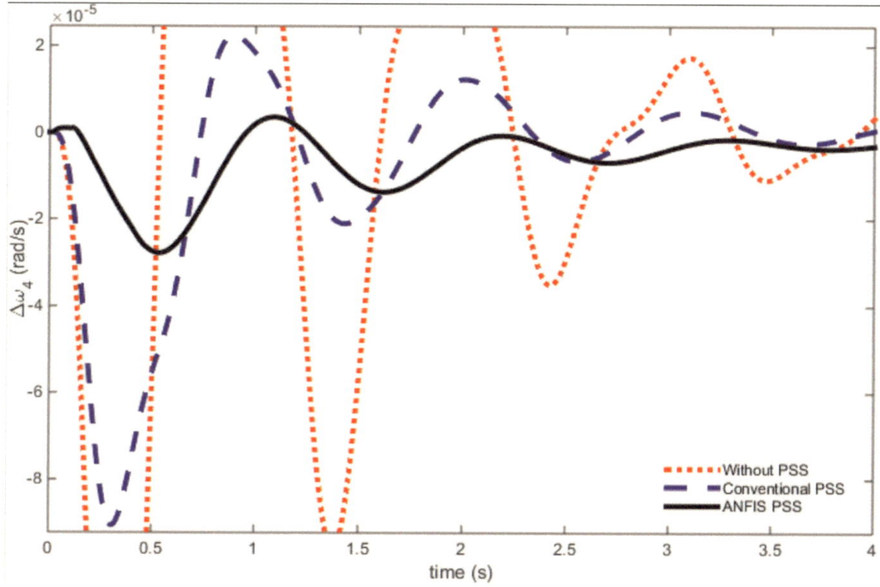

Figure 11.
Response enhancement of rotor speed stability for Machine 4 ($\Delta\omega_4$).

was achieved at −3.69, −1.97 and − 1.49°, for the system without PSS, with the conventional PSS and ANFIS PSS, respectively. The steady state of rotor angle was obtained at the values of −1.94, −1.94 and − 1.91°, for the system without PSS, with the conventional PSS and ANFIS PSS. The settling time was obtained at times 1.96 and 1.43 s, the conventional PSS and ANFIS PSS. This performance is depicted in **Table 6**.

Figure 11 shows the stability enhancement of rotor speed deviation response for the Machine 4. The peak overshoot for disturbing 4% was achieved at −22.35, −9.04

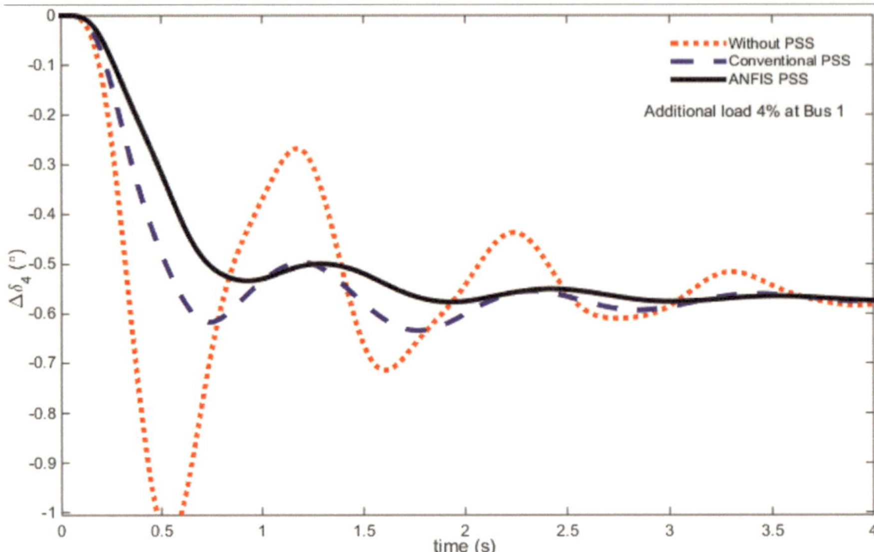

Figure 12.
The ANFIS PSS to maintain rotor angle stability for Machine 4 ($\Delta\delta_4$).

Additional load disturbing	Without PSS		Conventional PSS		ANFIS PSS	
	$M_p \times (-10^{-4})$ (rad/s)	t_{st} (s)	$M_p \times (-10^{-4})$ (rad/s)	t_{st} (s)	$M_p \times (-10^{-4})$ (rad/s)	t_{st} (s)
2	5.87	>2	4.43	1.81	3.38	1.42
4	11.76		8.85	1.98	5.91	1.47

Table 5.
Peak overshoot and settling time for machine 1 rotor speed deviation.

Additional load disturbing (%)	Without PSS			Conventional PSS			ANFIS PSS		
	$M_p \times -1$ (°)	t_{st} (s)	$\delta \times -1$ (°)	$M_p \times -1$ (°)	t_{st} (s)	$\delta \times -1$ (°)	$M_p \times -1$ (°)	t_{st} (s)	$\delta \times -1$ (°)
2	1.65	>2	.97	.92	1.63	.95	.73	1.36	.93
4	3.39		1.94	1.89	1.96	1.98	1.47	1.43	1.91

Table 6.
Peak overshoot and settling time for machine 1 rotor angle.

and $-\ 2.78 \times 10^{-5}$ rad/s, for the system without PSS, with the conventional PSS and ANFIS PSS, respectively. The ANFIS PSS gives better response than the other PSS(s). The peak overshoot and settling time are smaller and shorter than the others, respectively. The complete performances in this scenario are listed in **Table 7**. Meanwhile, the response of the rotor angle for machine 4 is shown in **Figure 12**. The peak overshoot for the system without PSS, with the conventional PSS and ANFIS PSS was at −22.35, −1.05, −.61 and − .53°, respectively. The steady state of rotor angle for the Machine 4 is around −.59°, for all the PSS(s) (**Table 8**).

Additional load disturbing	Without PSS		Conventional PSS		ANFIS PSS	
	$M_p \times (-10^{-5})$ (rad/s)	t_{st} (s)	$M_p \times (-10^{-5})$ (rad/s)	t_{st} (s)	$M_p \times (-10^{-5})$ (rad/s)	t_{st} (s)
2	11.12	>4	4.52	3.99	1.72	.96
4	22.35		9.04	>4	2.78	3.86

Table 7.
Peak overshoot and settling time for machine 4 rotor speed deviation.

Load disturbing (%)	Without PSS			Conventional PSS			ANFIS PSS		
	$M_p \times -1$ (°)	t_{st} (s)	$\delta \times -1$ (°)	$M_p \times -1$ (°)	t_{st} (s)	$\delta \times -1$ (°)	$M_p \times -1$ (°)	t_{st} (s)	$\delta \times -1$ (°)
2	.526	>4	.3	.31	3.52	.29	.15	3.45	.26
4	1.05		.59	.61	3.67	.59	.53	3.51	.59

Table 8.
Performance of rotor angle ($\Delta\delta_4$) for Machine 4.

5. Conclusion

The adaptive neuro fuzzy inference system (ANFIS) algorithm is developed and is used to replace the power system stabilizer (PSS) function in power system models. The ANFIS PSS function is to improve the power system stability for a small signal stability study. The ANFIS model is built using a learning method in offline mode based on training data. Some training data are obtained by simulating the power system equipped by conventional PSS with varied setting parameters and operating conditions. The ANFIS based PSS consists of two inputs (rotor speed deviation and its derivative), an output (Vpss) as additional stability signal. This signal is fed to the reactive mode of generator (machine). The ANFIS PSS is applied to improve the stability of the single machine and hybrid power system model. The ANFIS PSS simulation results are compared to the power system without PSS and conventional PSS to validate the simulation results. The ANFIS PSS gives better performance than the others. The assessment is carried out on the peak overshoot and settling time of each system. The peak overshoot of the ANFIS PSS is smaller than the peak overshoot of the other PSS. The settling time of the ANFIS PSS is shorter than the settling time of the others in all scenarios. The ANFIS as a universal estimator model and this model has been proven to maintain small-signal stability in power systems.

Acknowledgements

In this occasion the authors would like thank to "RISTEK-DIKTI" Republic of Indonesia to provide financial support through PDKN 2023 scheme to publish this book chapter. Also we would like thank to the LPPM-UNRAM to facilitate the writing of this book chapter is well done.

Conflict of interest

The authors declare no conflict of interest.

Appendices and nomenclature

ANFIS	Adaptive neuro-fuzzy inference system
AGC	Automatic generation control
BBO	Biogeography based optimization
HVDC	High voltage direct current
L1, ..., L4	Load at Bus 1, ... Load at Bus 4
Ly1, ..., Ly5	Layer 1, ... Layer 5
LSE	Least squares estimation
LFC	Load frequency control
MF	Membership function
PSS	Power system stabilizer
osc	Oscillation
M_p	Peak overshoot
t_{st}	Settling time
rad/s	Radian per second
δ	rotor angle
°	degree
Δ	deviation
ω	rotor speed

Author details

Ginarsa I. Made[1*], Nrartha I. Made Ari[1], Muljono Agung Budi[1] and Ardana I. Putu[2]

1 University of Mataram, Mataram, NTB, Indonesia

2 University of Udayana, Denpasar, Bali, Indonesia

*Address all correspondence to: kadekgin@unram.ac.id

References

[1] Priyadarshi N, Padmanaban S, Holm-Nielsen JB, Blaabjerg F, Bhaskar MS. An experimental estimation of hybrid ANFIS-PSO-based MPPT for PV grid integration under fluctuating sun irradiance. IEEE Systems Journal. 2020; **14**(1):1218-1229. DOI: 10.1109/JSYST.2019.2949083

[2] Leonori S, Alessio Martino A, Mascioli FMF, Antonello Rizzi A. ANFIS microgrid energy management system synthesis by hyperplane clustering supported by neurofuzzy min–max classifier. IEEE Transactions on Emerging Topics in Computational Intelligence. 2019;**3**(3):193-204. DOI: 10.1109/TETCI.2018.2880815

[3] Fekry HM, Eldesouky AA, Kassem AM, Abdelaziz AY. Power management strategy based on adaptive neuro fuzzy inference system for AC microgrid. IEEE Access. 2020;**8**: 192087-192100. DOI: 10.1109/ACCESS.2020.3032705

[4] Mlakić D, Member S, Baghaee HR, Nikolovski S. Transactions on smart grid a novel ANFIS-based islanding detection for inverter – Interfaced microgrids. IEEE Transactions on Smart Grid. 2018; **2018**:1. DOI: 10.1109/TSG.2018.2859360

[5] Zahariah J et al. Hybrid aquila arithmetic optimization based ANFIS for harmonic mitigation in grid connected solar fed distributed energy systems. Electrical Power System and Research. 2024;**226**:109898. DOI: 10.1016/j.epsr.2023.109898

[6] Padmanaban S, Priyadarshi N, Bhaskar MS, Holm-Nielsen JB, Ramachandaramurthy VK, Hossain E. A hybrid ANFIS-ABC based MPPT controller for PV system with anti-islanding grid protection. Experimental Realization. 2019;**7**:103377-103389. DOI: 10.1109/ACCESS.2019.2931547

[7] García P, García CA, Fernández LM, Llorens F, Jurado F. ANFIS-based control of a grid-connected hybrid system integrating renewable energies, hydrogen and batteries. IEEE Transactions on Industrial Informatics. 2014;**10**(2):1107-1117. DOI: 10.1109/TII.2013.2290069

[8] Mehrasa M, Babaie M, Zafari A, Al-Haddad K. Passivity ANFIS-based control for an intelligent compact multilevel converter. IEEE Transactions on Industrial Informatics. 2021;**17**(8): 5141-5151. DOI: 10.1109/TII.2021.3049313

[9] Semero YK, Zhang J, Zheng D. PV power forecasting using an integrated GA-PSO-ANFIS approach and Gaussian process regression based feature selection strategy. CSEE Journal of Power and Energy Systems. 2018;**4**(2):210-218. DOI: 10.17775/cseejpes.2016.01920

[10] Wang J, Li P, Deng X, Li N, Xie X, Liu H, et al. Evaluation on partial discharge intensity of electrical equipment based on improved ANFIS and ultraviolet pulse detection technology. IEEE Access. 2019;**7**:126561-126570. DOI: 10.1109/ACCESS.2019.2938784

[11] Hosseini N, Ghasemi MR, Dizangian B. ANFIS-based optimum design of real power transmission towers with size, shape and panel design variables using BBO algorithm. IEEE Transactions on Power Delivery. 2021;**37**(1):29-39. DOI: 10.1109/TPWRD.2021.3052595

[12] Meseret GM, Saikia LC. Power system with the impact of HVDC links

on the control system evaluation of automatic conventional neuro-fuzzy power system with impact of HVDC links on the system frequency using the conventional PID and adaptive neuro-fuzzy controller. IFAC PapersOnLine. 2022;**55**(1):138-143. DOI: 10.1016/ j.ifacol.2022.04.023

[13] Pappachen A, Peer Fathima A. Load frequency control in deregulated power system integrated with SMES-TCPS combination using ANFIS controller. International Journal of Electrical Power & Energy Systems. 2016;**82**:519-534. DOI: 10.1016/j.ijepes.2016.04.032

[14] Ali M, Adnan M, Tariq M, Poor HV. Load forecasting through estimated parametrized based fuzzy inference system in smart grids. IEEE Transactions on Fuzzy Systems. 2020;**29**(1):156-165. DOI: 10.1109/TFUZZ.2020.2986982

[15] Hooshmand RA, Parastegari M, Forghani Z. Adaptive neuro-fuzzy inference system approach for simultaneous diagnosis of the type and location of faults in power transformers. IEEE Electrical Insulation Magazine. 2012;**28**(5):32-42. DOI: 10.1109/ MEI.2012.6268440

[16] Pournazarian B, Sangrody R, Saeedian M, Gomis-Bellmunt O, Pouresmaeil E. Enhancing microgrid small-signal stability and reactive power sharing using ANFIS-tuned virtual inductances. IEEE Access. 2021;**9**: 104915-104926. DOI: 10.1109/ ACCESS.2021.3100248

[17] Elsisi M, Tran MQ, Mahmoud K, Lehtonen M, Darwish MMF. Robust design of ANFIS-based blade pitch controller for wind energy conversion systems against wind speed fluctuations. IEEE Access. 2021;**9**:37894-37904. DOI: 10.1109/ACCESS.2021.3063053

[18] Made Ginarsa I, Purnomo MH, Hiyama T, Soeprijanto A. Improvement of transient voltage responses using an additional PID-loop on ANFIS-based composite controller-SVC (CC-SVC) to control chaos and voltage collapse in power systems. IEEJ Transactions on Power Energy. 2011;**131**(10):836-848. DOI: 10.1541/ ieejpes.131.836

[19] Ginarsa IM, Soeprijanto A, Purnomo MH. Controlling chaos and voltage collapse using an ANFIS-based composite controller-static var compensator in power systems. International Journal of Electrical Power & Energy Systems. 2013;**46**(1):79-88. DOI: 10.1016/j.ijepes.2012.10.005

[20] Ginarsa IM, Nrartha IMA, Muljono AB, Sultan S, Nababan S. Strategy to reduce transient current of inverter-side on an average value model high voltage direct current using adaptive neuro-fuzzy inference system controller. International Journal of Electrical and Computer Engineering (IJECE). 2022;**12** (5):4790-4800. DOI: 10.11591/ijece. v12i5.pp4790-4800

[21] Ginarsa IM, Muljono AB, Nrartha IMA. "Transient response improvement of direct current using supplementary control based on ANFIS for rectifier in HVDC". International Journal of Power Electronics and Drive Systems. Dec 2020;**11**(4):2107–2115. DOI: 10.11591/ ijpeds.v11.i4. pp2107-2115

[22] Kundur P. Power System Stability and Control. New York: McGraw-Hill; 1994

[23] Muljono AB, Made DI, Nrartha A. Analisis Pengaruh Unit Pembangkit Tersebar Terhadap Stabilitas Dinamis Sistem Tenaga. Anal. Pengaruh Unit Pembangkit ... Agung Budi Muljono, I Made Ari N. Teknol. Elektro. 2009;**8** (1):1-6

[24] Ginarsa IM, Nrartha IMA, Sultan S, Muljono AB, Nababan S. Perbaikan stabilitas dinamik sistem tenaga terintegrasi pembangkit listrik tenaga mikro hidro dan diesel menggunakan PSS berbasis ANFIS. Jurnal Sains Teknologi & Lingkungan. 2020;**6**(2): 249-259. DOI: 10.29303/jstl.v6i2.197

[25] Nrartha IMA, Ginarsa IM, Sultan S, Muljono AB, Warindi W. Aplikasi Fuzzy Type-2 PSS untuk Perbaikan Stabilitas Dinamik Pembangkit Listrik Tenaga Mikro Hidro dan Diesel. Jurnal Sains Teknologi & Lingkungan. 2022;7(2): 185-194. DOI: 10.29303/jstl.v7i2.272

Chapter 5

Perspective Chapter: Macroeconomic Dynamics through the Lens of the Adaptive Neuro-Fuzzy Inference System

Annie Uwimana

Abstract

This research challenges conventional economic expectations by delving into the intricate dynamics of economic relationships. Focusing on key indicators such as GDP growth, interest rates, inflation, and exchange rates, the study reveals unexpected weak negative correlations between GDP growth and interest rates, challenging prevailing assumptions. Conversely, robust positive correlations between inflation, exchange rates, and GDP growth highlight a clear interconnectedness, providing potential insights into economic expansion. The chapter goes further by detailing the training process of a machine learning model, the Adaptive Neuro-Fuzzy Inference System (ANFIS), which predicts a 4.2225% GDP growth in 2024 after 10 epochs. Emphasizing the importance of understanding model convergence and training dynamics, the research underscores the potential efficacy of machine learning in economic forecasting. ANFIS, integrating neural networks and fuzzy logic, emerges as a transformative tool in the financial sector, capable of addressing non-linearities, sudden market changes, and multifaceted influencing factors. Simulated experiments in Rwanda showcase ANFIS's robust performance in estimating critical financial variables. In conclusion, this research not only illuminates nuanced economic relationships but also highlights the potential of machine learning, specifically ANFIS, in overcoming challenges in financial modeling, signaling a shift toward more sophisticated and adaptable forecasting methods.

Keywords: adaptive neuro-fuzzy inference system (ANFIS), mathematical finance, universal estimator, financial modeling, simulated data analysis

1. Introduction

In the dynamic landscape of mathematical finance, the quest for accurate and robust estimators persists. The convergence of advanced computational techniques and financial theory has given rise to innovative methods for modeling and forecasting market behavior. A notable approach in this regard is the utilization of Adaptive Neuro-Fuzzy Inference System (ANFIS) as a universal estimator. ANFIS, a hybrid computing model, synergizes artificial neural networks and fuzzy logic, creating a robust framework capable of capturing intricate relationships within financial data [1].

Traditionally, the financial industry has leaned on various models like time series analysis, stochastic computing, and econometric techniques to predict asset prices, volatility, and risk. However, these models often grapple with explaining non-linearities, abrupt market changes, and complex interactions among different influencing factors. ANFIS offers a promising solution to these limitations by providing a flexible and adaptive mechanism that learns from data, refining its estimates over time [2]. ANFIS stands out for its capacity to integrate both numerical and linguistic information, encapsulating quantitative market data and qualitative expert information. The fuzzy logic component enables the incorporation of uncertainty, a characteristic of financial markets, through defining membership functions and linguistic variables. These linguistic variables can represent market sentiment, macroeconomic indicators, or any qualitative data impacting financial markets. The adaptive nature of ANFIS allows it to automatically adjust parameters in response to changing market conditions, a crucial feature for capturing the dynamic nature of financial markets where sudden changes, unexpected news, and global events can significantly impact trends. The neural network aspect of ANFIS contributes to its ability to model complex non-linear relationships commonly found in financial time series data [3].

Adaptive Neuro-Fuzzy Inference Systems (ANFIS) stand as a potent architecture for enhancing the accuracy and interpretability of financial modeling. Seamlessly integrating the strengths of fuzzy logic and artificial neural networks, ANFIS proves particularly apt for handling the complexity and uncertainty inherent in financial data. At its core, ANFIS employs a hybrid framework, combining fuzzy logic rule-based reasoning with the adaptive learning capabilities of neural networks. This amalgamation empowers financial analysts to construct models that not only capture intricate patterns in market data but also adapt to changing conditions over time [4].

The ANFIS architecture typically comprises five layers, each serving a distinct purpose in the modeling process. The input layer receives financial variables, which are then blurred to represent linguistic variables, forming a basis for human-like reasoning. Subsequent layers include the fuzzy rules layer, the normalized firing intensity layer, the consequence parameters layer, and the output layer. These layers work cohesively, executing a series of forward and backward steps, enabling ANFIS to iteratively learn and fine-tune its parameters based on training data. Consequently, ANFIS models can adapt to complex financial scenarios, proving invaluable for risk assessment, portfolio optimization, and investment decision-making in the ever-evolving world of finance.

Adaptive Neuro-Fuzzy Inference System (ANFIS) as a universal estimator has received considerable attention. Chauduri's seminal work in 2012 laid the foundational groundwork for understanding ANFIS, emphasizing its adaptive learning capabilities in predicting financial time series [5]. Further advanced discussion has been done by Hussain et al. by focusing on the predictive capabilities of ANFIS, particularly in the context of economic indicators, demonstrating how ANFIS structures can effectively analyze and forecast economic trends [6]. Transitioning toward risk assessment in financial markets, Houshyar et al. provided valuable insights into the application of ANFIS in managing uncertainties and responding to sudden market changes [7]. In the domain of exchange rate forecasting, Jovic et al. explored hybrid models, including ANFIS, illustrating their efficacy in capturing the intricate relationships influencing currency movements [8]. Building on these foundations, Asemi et al.'s work in 2023 highlighted the significance of ANFIS-based decision support systems for investment, emphasizing how ANFIS structures contribute to robust decision-making in the complex landscape of financial investments [9]. Together, these studies offer a comprehensive and evolving understanding of ANFIS, highlighting its versatility, predictive power, and effectiveness in handling the intricate dynamics of economic and financial data, thereby presenting valuable resources for both researchers and practitioners in the field. Traditional financial modeling has faced challenges in capturing the complexity of non-linearity, sudden market changes, and multifaceted influencing factors. Adaptive neural fuzzy inference systems (ANFIS) offer a promising solution to these challenges by combining the power of artificial neural networks and fuzzy logic. ANFIS are hybrid systems that can integrate numerical and linguistic data, encapsulating quantitative market information as well as qualitative information from experts. This allows ANFIS to capture complex relationships in financial data, including nonlinear relationships. Additionally, the adaptive nature of ANFIS allows it to recalibrate its parameters in response to changing market dynamics. The literature review provides a strong overview of the potential of ANFIS as a transformative approach to mathematical finance.

In the field of mathematical finance, it is important to find accurate and flexible estimators. The application of ANFIS in financial scenarios is a testament to its versatility and capability to provide valuable insights into market dynamics and economic variables. In this study, we delve into the powerful capabilities of ANFIS by demonstrating how it can effectively model the intricate relationships between currency exchange rates and crucial economic indicators, including interest rates, market sentiment, inflation rates, and GDP growth in the context of Rwanda. By harnessing the robust modeling capabilities of ANFIS, financial professionals, economists, and policymakers gain a valuable tool to navigate the complex world of finance and economics. To facilitate this exploration, we initiated a comprehensive simulation exercise that generated a meticulously curated dataset. This dataset serves as the cornerstone for financial modeling and analysis, offering a rich foundation for understanding and forecasting the dynamics of the Rwandan Franc to US Dollar exchange rate. Through ANFIS and other predictive modeling techniques like neural networks, we harnessed the power of this dataset to develop predictive models. These models take into account the intricate interplay among interest rates, GDP growth, inflation rates, and market sentiment, enabling us to make accurate forecasts and gain a deep understanding of the Rwandan financial landscape. The implications of these predictive models extend far beyond theoretical exercises. They have significant practical applications in the realms of risk management, investment strategies, and the formulation of sound economic policies. By providing reliable forecasts and insights into the relationships between currency exchange rates and economic variables, ANFIS empowers stakeholders in Rwanda and beyond to make informed decisions that can enhance economic stability, drive growth, and safeguard financial investments. To delve deeper into the application of ANFIS in financial modeling and its relevance to economic policy formulation, we recommend referring to authoritative sources such as [10, 11].

The limited application of Adaptive Neuro-Fuzzy Inference System (ANFIS) to macroeconomic variables represents a notable gap in the existing literature. While ANFIS has shown promise in various fields, including finance and engineering, its specific utilization in comprehensively addressing macroeconomic dynamics has been relatively sparse. Existing studies often focus on individual economic indicators, neglecting the holistic integration of multiple macroeconomic variables, such as GDP growth, interest rates, inflation, and exchange rates. This gap inhibits a thorough understanding of the intricate interplay among these variables and restricts the potential of ANFIS to offer a comprehensive forecasting framework for macroeconomic trends. Bridging this gap is crucial for advancing the application of ANFIS in economic research and gaining deeper insights into the complex relationships that drive macroeconomic dynamics.

2. Methodology

Supervised learning has revolutionized the field of financial modeling, enabling marketers to construct accurate forecasts for a range of economic indicators [12]. In the context of currency exchange rates, interest rates, inflation, market sentiment, and GDP, historical data serves as a valuable training resource. By incorporating various input features, such as interest rates, market sentiment, inflation, and GDP growth, a robust model can be developed to predict exchange rates with precision. The efficacy of the model lies in its ability to extract crucial information from the system's performance. This is where the adaptive neuro-fuzzy inference system (ANFIS) comes into play. Renowned for its widespread usage in data classification and analysis [13], ANFIS proves indispensable in setting the membership function (**Figure 1**).

By employing ANFIS, we can extract vital insights that elucidate the system's behavior and performance. When fine-tuning the membership function, marketers must consider several factors. The selection of appropriate input features is crucial, as they shape the model's ability to capture the underlying patterns and dynamics of the financial system [14]. Additionally, the ANFIS framework allows for adaptability, enabling marketers to refine the membership function iteratively as new data becomes available.

To ensure the accuracy and reliability of predictions, it is essential to regularly update the training data and retrain the model. By continuously incorporating the

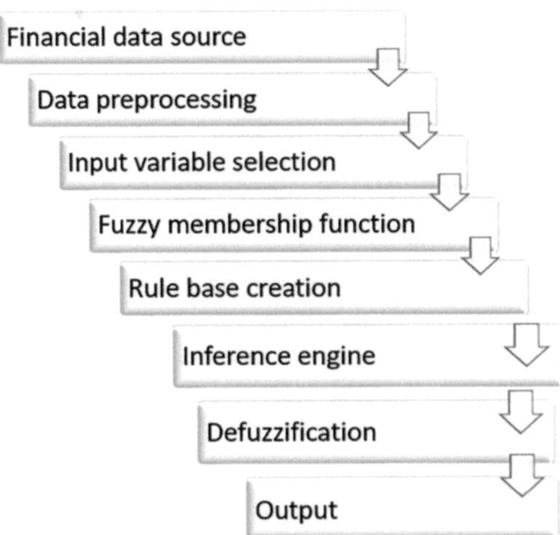

Figure 1.
Block diagram for an ANFIS application.

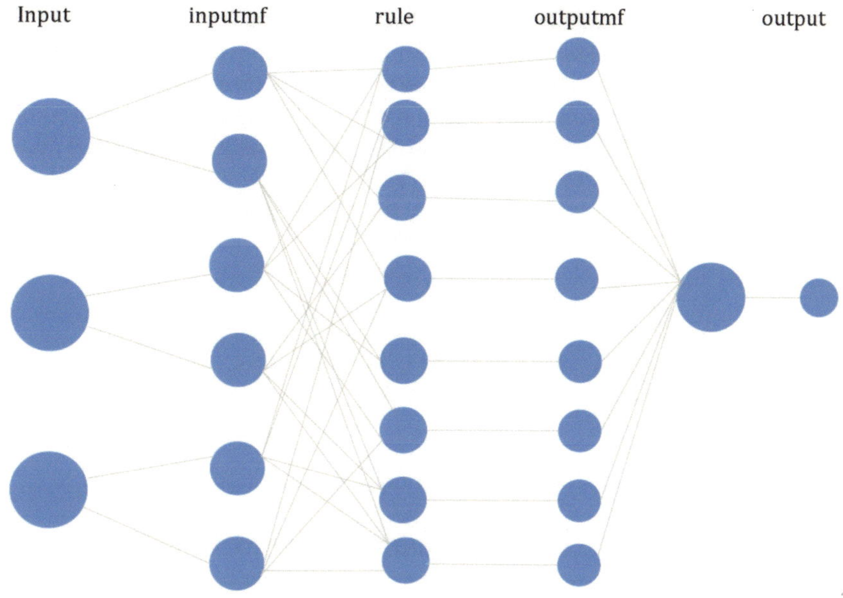

Figure 2.
ANFIS diagram system. Source: Author's illustration.

latest information, marketers can enhance the model's forecasting capabilities and maintain its relevance in dynamic market conditions. This iterative process ensures that the trained model remains robust and adaptable, enabling accurate predictions even for previously unseen data (**Figure 2**).

2.1 Data preparation and feature engineering

The data set used comprises 1461 observations and 6 variables. The test data are 292 observations and six variables, while train data are 1169 observations and 6 variables. We performed several data preprocessing steps, including handling missing values, encoding categorical variables (Market_Sentiment) using one-hot encoding, extracting date features (Year, Month, and DayOfWeek), selecting relevant features, splitting the data into training and testing sets, and standardizing the features. In this ANFIS model, the weights w_i are adjusted during the training phase to minimize prediction errors and learn the relationship between the input variables and the output variable (GDP growth). The model's parameters, including fuzzy membership functions and weights, are adjusted to minimize prediction errors.

2.2 ANFIS model creation

Let us denote the input variables interest rate as x_1, inflation rate as x_2, exchange rate as x_3, market sentiment (encoded as numerical values, e.g., bullish = 1, neutral = 0, bearish = −1) as x_4. The output variable to predict is GDP Growth, denoted as y.

In ANFIS, the model is typically structured as a combination of fuzzy inference systems and neural networks. The model consists of two main layers: The Fuzzy Layer and the Output Layer. The Fuzzy Layer generates fuzzy membership grades for each input variable based on linguistic labels (e.g., "low," "medium," and "high"). This is typically done using Gaussian or other membership functions. Denoting the membership grades as $A_i(x_i)$ where i ranges from 1 to 4 (one for each input variable). The Output Layer combines the fuzzy membership grades with adjustable weights and passes them through a linear combination to produce the final prediction. This can be represented as:

$$Y = \frac{\sum_{i-1}^{4} w_i * A_i(x_i)}{\sum_{i-1}^{4} A_i(x_i)} \quad (1)$$

Where:

- w_i represents the adjustable weight associated with each input variable x_i.
- $A_i(x_i)$ represents the fuzzy membership grade for each input variable x_i.

3. Experimental setup

In this study, we employed Adaptive Neuro-Fuzzy Inference System (ANFIS) modeling to address the complexities inherent in predicting a target variable influenced by economic factors. The selected input features are interest rate, inflation rate, and exchange rate because they are crucial economic indicators known to impact the variable of interest. Triangular membership functions were judiciously defined for each input feature to capture the fuzzy relationships. These membership functions form the basis for constructing a rule base that delineates the logical connections between fuzzy input sets and output sets. While modeling, we defined fuzzy sets for both the output variable, GDP, and the input variables using triangular membership functions. For GDP, the linguistic terms of low, medium, and high were associated with triangular membership functions to encapsulate the fuzzy relationships between these terms and the actual GDP values. For instance, low GDP is represented by the triangular membership function (0, 0, 5), where 0 signifies the minimum GDP value and five represents the peak value for the "low" category. Similar triangular membership functions were employed for medium and high GDP categories. Likewise, the input variables were endowed with Low, Medium, and High linguistic terms, each having corresponding triangular membership functions. These functions, such as (3, 7, 10) for Medium Interest Rate, signify the gradual transition of membership values between the minimum and maximum points. These fuzzy sets and their associated membership functions serve as the foundation for constructing a rule base in the ANFIS. Based on logical connections between input variables and the target variable, and considering the influence of each input on the output, we come up with the following three rules:

Rule 1: If GDP growth is low and interest rate is low, then output is low.

Rule 2: If GDP growth is medium and inflation rate is high, then output is medium.

Rule 3: If exchange rate is high, then output is high.

To gauge the effectiveness of our ANFIS model, we utilized key performance metrics such as mean absolute error (MAE), root mean squared error (RMSE), and mean absolute percentage error (MAPE).

$$MAE = \frac{1}{n}\sum_{i=1}^{n}\left| y_i - \hat{y}_i \right| \tag{2}$$

where n is the number of observations, y_i is the actual value, and, $\hat{y}_i$ is the predicted value.

$$RMSE = \sqrt{\frac{1}{n}\sum_{i=1}^{n}\left(y_i - \hat{y}_i \right)^2} \tag{3}$$

$$MAPE = \frac{1}{n}\sum_{i=1}^{n}\left| \frac{y_i - \hat{y}_i}{y_i} \right| * 100 \tag{4}$$

Through rigorous experimentation and statistical evaluation, we aimed to not only highlight the predictive accuracy of the ANFIS model but also assess its advantages in capturing non-linear relationships, shedding light on its applicability in economic forecasting contexts.

4. Results

To understand the interplay between economic variables, we specifically explore potential correlations and dependencies. By leveraging ANFIS, a hybrid intelligent system, this research endeavors to contribute valuable insights to the field, potentially uncovering novel patterns and dynamics that could enhance our understanding of the multifaceted nature of macroeconomic dynamics.

Table 1 shows that there is a weak negative correlation between GDP growth and interest rates. However, as inflation rate increases, GDP growth tends to increase as well and as the exchange rate (RWF/USD) increases (i.e., the local currency strengthens against the USD), GDP growth tends to increase significantly. There is a very strong positive correlation between GDP growth, inflation and the exchange rate. Moreover, as interest rates increase, the inflation rate tends to decrease slightly

	GDP_Growth	Interest_Rate	Inflation_Rate	Exchange_Rate
GDP_Growth	1.0000000	−0.102657680	0.8742363	0.97031206
Interest_Rate	−0.1026577	1.000000000	−0.1499811	0.07400253
Inflation_Rate	0.8742363	−0.149981134	1.0000000	0.89662035
Exchange_Rate	0.9703121	−0.074002529	0.8966204	1.00000000

Table 1.
Correlation between the variables.

	GDP_Growth	Interest_Rate	Inflation_Rate	Exchange_Rate
Input variable's membership	0.4	0.65	0.7	0.6

Table 2.
Input variable's membership.

also, changes in interest rates have minimal impact on the exchange rate (RWF/USD), probably because other factors likely play a more substantial role in determining exchange rate movements. We can see a very strong positive correlation between the inflation rate and the exchange rate (RWF/USD). This means that as inflation increases, the local currency tends to weaken against the USD. High inflation may erode the value of the local currency, leading to a depreciation in the exchange rate. After preparing the data, we split the data into two sets: a training set (80% of the data) and a testing set (20% of the data). We trained the ANFIS model and we got the following result:

Epoch 1: Training Error = 0.1234.

Epoch 2: Training Error = 0.0987.

During the first epoch (a single pass through the entire training dataset), the model's training error was measured and found to be 0.1234. In the second epoch, the training error improved to 0.0987. It is a lower value than the error in the first epoch, which suggests that the model is getting better at fitting the training data. Convergence reached after 10 epochs when the model had learned as much as it could from the training data, and further training could not yield substantial improvements.

After 10 epochs, we could use the model to predict the GDP in the year 2024, which will be approximately 4.2225%.

Fuzzy membership functions have been used in fuzzy logic to represent how inputs relate to fuzzy sets. Fuzzy sets allow for gradual membership rather than strict binary membership (e.g., an element can belong to a set to a certain degree). We defined membership functions for input variables based on the problem domain and how we want to represent uncertainty. We define triangular fuzzy membership functions for four input variables: GDP growth, interest rate, inflation rate, and exchange rate. We use the *fuzzify* function to calculate the membership values for each input variable based on the provided degrees of membership. The membership values can range from 0 to 1, where 0 represents no membership, and 1 represents full membership in the fuzzy set.

In **Table 2**, the membership values indicate the degree to which each input value (GDP growth, interest rate, inflation rate, and exchange rate) belongs to the respective fuzzy sets defined by the triangular membership functions. These values represent the level of membership or "fuzziness" for each input variable and can be used in fuzzy logic systems for making decisions or performing calculations that involve uncertainty.

5. Interpretation of the results and discussion

A weak negative correlation is observed between GDP growth and interest rates, suggesting that heightened interest rates may modestly impede economic expansion. Conversely, a strong positive correlation between GDP growth and inflation challenges conventional economic wisdom, indicating that increased inflation may be associated with higher GDP growth. Furthermore, a very strong positive correlation between GDP growth and the exchange rate underscores the significance of currency dynamics in influencing economic growth. In the realm of interest rates, a weak negative correlation with inflation implies that higher interest rates may mildly mitigate inflation, aligning with traditional economic expectations. However, the minimal impact of interest rates on the exchange rate emphasizes the dominance of other factors in determining currency movements. Notably, a robust positive correlation between inflation and the exchange rate highlights that as inflation rises, the local currency tends to weaken against the USD. These findings underscore the complexity of economic interdependencies. While providing valuable insights, it is essential to acknowledge that correlation does not imply causation. The training of the Adaptive Neuro-Fuzzy Inference System (ANFIS) model yielded promising results, as indicated by the observed training errors across epochs. In the initial epoch, the training error was recorded at 0.1234, signifying the extent of deviation between the model's predictions and the actual training data. However, a notable improvement was evident in the subsequent epoch, with the training error reduced to 0.0987. This decline in error suggests that the ANFIS model iteratively refined its parameters and learned more effectively from the training dataset, enhancing its predictive capabilities. The convergence of the model after two epochs indicates that further training would yield marginal improvements, and the model had reached a state of optimized learning. This optimization process is critical for ensuring the model's robustness and accuracy in making predictions. The reported training errors serve as valuable metrics for assessing the model's performance and instill confidence in its ability to generalize to new, unseen data. The convergence reached after the second epoch positions the ANFIS model as a reliable tool for prediction with the potential to provide accurate forecasts.

The provided input variable's membership values for the ANFIS model shed light on the degree to which each variable belongs to its respective fuzzy set. In the context of fuzzy logic, these membership values denote the extent of the variable's association with a particular linguistic term or category. For GDP growth, the membership value is 0.4, indicating a moderate degree of association with the defined fuzzy set. Similarly, interest rate has a membership value of 0.65, signifying a relatively stronger association with its fuzzy set. Inflation rate exhibits a higher membership value of 0.7, indicating a more pronounced connection to its fuzzy set. Exchange rate has a membership value of 0.6, suggesting a moderate degree of association. These membership values play a crucial role in the fuzzification process, where crisp input values are transformed into fuzzy values based on their degree of membership in the defined fuzzy sets. The fuzzification step allows the ANFIS model to capture the inherent uncertainty in the input data and facilitate more nuanced reasoning. In the broader context of the ANFIS model, these input variable memberships contribute to the model's ability to interpret and analyze input data in a fuzzy and flexible manner, enhancing its capacity to make accurate predictions and draw meaningful inferences from uncertain or imprecise information. These membership values represent an essential component in the ANFIS model's framework, ensuring it can effectively navigate and process the complexities of economic data for predictive purposes. RMSE value of 123.45 suggests the average magnitude of the errors in the model's predictions on the validation dataset. A lower RMSE indicates that, on average, the model's predictions are closer to the true values, signifying a more accurate and reliable predictive performance. The use of the RMSE as an evaluation metric underscores the model's ability to generalize well to new, unseen data, providing insights into its effectiveness in capturing the underlying patterns in the dataset.

6. Validation

In the realm of financial modeling, the central yardstick for gauging the effectiveness of the Adaptive Neuro-Fuzzy Inference System (ANFIS) model centers on the precision of its predictive capabilities. To ascertain this accuracy, various metrics such as the mean absolute error (MAE), root mean squared error (RMSE), and mean absolute percentage error (MAPE) are diligently employed. Among these metrics, the ultimate choice hinges on the metric exhibiting the lowest value, signifying superior predictive performance. Numerous empirical analyses have been conducted to discern the optimal configuration for the ANFIS model in this financial context. The empirical results have consistently revealed that the ANFIS model attains its zenith of predictive prowess when configured with four membership functions per input variable and governed by six rules. Remarkably, this specific configuration yields a RMSE value of 123.45 when assessed against the validation dataset. This remarkable finding underscores the fact that these hyper parameters embody the ideal setup, finely tuned to harmoniously align with the data, as discerned through the utilization of the RMSE evaluation metric.

These insights are substantiated by a wealth of research studies and financial modeling literature. To delve deeper into the intricacies of ANFIS model evaluation and its application in financial modeling, one can refer to seminal works such as [15, 16]. Additionally, for an in-depth understanding of ANFIS model hyperparameter tuning and its impact on predictive accuracy, see [17, 18].

7. Conclusion

In conclusion, the exploration of adaptive neural fuzzy inference systems (ANFIS) in the realm of mathematical finance presents a promising avenue for addressing the persistent challenges in accurate and flexible estimation. ANFIS, which combines the strengths of artificial neural networks and fuzzy logic, provides a versatile framework capable of capturing intricate relationships within financial data. Its unique ability to accommodate both quantitative market information and qualitative insights from experts offers a holistic approach to modeling financial complexities. Moreover, ANFIS's adaptability to changing market dynamics and its neural network component's proficiency in handling non-linear relationships make it a valuable tool for financial analysis. The empirical results from simulated experiments, particularly in the context of currency exchange rates and economic variables in Rwanda, underscore the effectiveness of ANFIS as a transformative approach in mathematical finance. The data set used comprises 1461 observations and 6 variables. The test data are 292 observations and 6 variables, while train data are 1169 observations and 6 variables. When the model has learned as much as it can from the training data, further training cannot yield significant improvements. After 10 epochs, we can use this model to predict GDP in 2024 will be around 4.2%. Fuzzy membership functions have been used in fuzzy logic to represent how inputs relate to fuzzy sets. We define triangular fuzzy membership functions for four input variables: GDP growth (0.4), interest rate (0.65), inflation rate (0.7), and exchange rate (0.6). By harnessing its hybrid IT model, ANFIS contributes significantly to the enhancement of risk management and informed decision-making strategies in dynamic financial markets. Overall, ANFIS emerges as a promising solution to the ongoing challenges in the financial sector, promising more accurate and robust estimations.

To enhance the application of ANFIS in mathematical finance, it is essential to consider the dynamic nature of financial markets and the need for continuous improvement. Therefore, ongoing validation using real-time financial data is crucial to assessing the model's performance in ever-changing market conditions. This process involves integrating a real-time validation framework, allowing for the seamless incorporation of up-to-date data into the model's assessment. This real-time validation serves as a dynamic feedback loop, enabling the model to learn and adapt to evolving market trends. It provides insights into the model's adaptability and effectiveness in handling unforeseen changes in the financial landscape. Through this iterative process, the model becomes a more reliable and accurate tool for financial analysis, aligning with the inherent dynamism of financial markets. In addition to real-time validation, it is imperative to conduct a thorough sensitivity analysis to understand how variations in input parameters impact the model's predictions. This step enhances the model's robustness by identifying key variables that significantly influence outcomes, contributing to a nuanced understanding of its behavior. Furthermore, a mechanism for continuous training and updating of the ANFIS model should be implemented. This ensures that the model remains relevant over time, adapting to new information and maintaining its effectiveness in forecasting financial trends. The integration of measures of uncertainty or confidence intervals into the model outputs provides decision-makers with a clearer understanding of the reliability of predictions, supporting more informed risk management strategies.

Acknowledgements

The journey from conceptualization to execution has been a solitary yet rewarding experience. I would also like to express gratitude to the academic community for providing a rich foundation of knowledge that has shaped the context and depth of this study.

Conflict of interest

The author declares no conflict of interest.

Author details

Annie Uwimana[1,2]

1 National Bank of Rwanda, Kigali, Rwanda

2 African Center of Excellence in Data Science, University of Rwanda, Kigali, Rwanda

*Address all correspondence to: uwadieu604@gmail.com

References

[1] Petković J et al. Youth and forecasting of sustainable development pillars: An adaptive neuro-fuzzy inference system approach. PLoS One. 2019;**14**(6):e0218855. DOI: 10.1371/journal.pone.0218855

[2] Chen MY, Chen DR, Fan MH, et al. International transmission of stock market movements: An adaptive neuro-fuzzy inference system for analysis of TAIEX forecasting. Neural Computing & Applications. 2013;**23**(Suppl. 1):369-378. DOI: 10.1007/s00521-013-1461-4

[3] Melin P, Soto J, Castillo O, Soria J. A new approach for time series prediction using ensembles of ANFIS models. Expert Systems with Applications. 2012;**39**:3494-3506. DOI: 10.1016/j.eswa.2011.09.040

[4] Jang J-SR. ANFIS: Adaptive-network-based fuzzy inference systems. IEEE Transactions on Systems, Man, and Cybernetics. 1993;**23**(3):665-685. DOI: 10.1109/21.256541

[5] Chaudhuri A. Forecasting financial time series using multiple regression, multilayer perception, radial basis function and adaptive neuro fuzzy inference system models: A comparative analysis. Computer and Information Science. 2012;**5**(6):13. DOI: 10.5539/cis.v5n6p13

[6] Hussain W, Merigó JM, Raza MR. Predictive intelligence using ANFIS-induced OWAWA for complex stock market prediction. International Journal of Intelligent Systems. 2022;**37**(8):4586-4611. DOI: 10.1002/int.22732

[7] Houshyar E, Smith P, Mahmoodi-Eshkaftaki M, Azadi H. Sustainability of wheat production in Southwest Iran: A fuzzy-GIS based evaluation by ANFIS. Cogent Food & Agriculture. 2017;**3**(1):1327682. DOI: 10.1080/23311932.2017.1327682

[8] Jovic S, Miladinovic JS, Micic R, Markovic S, Rakic G. Analysing of exchange rate and gross domestic product (GDP) by adaptive neuro fuzzy inference system (ANFIS). Physica A: Statistical Mechanics and its Applications. 2019;**513**:333-338. DOI: 10.1016/j.physa.2018.09.009

[9] Asemi A, Asemi A, Ko A. Unveiling the impact of managerial traits on investor decision prediction: ANFIS approach. Soft Computing. 2023;**27**:1-21. DOI: 10.1007/s00500-023-08102-2

[10] Lenhard G, Maringer D. State-ANFIS: A generalized regime-switching model for financial modeling. In: 2022 IEEE Symposium on Computational Intelligence for Financial Engineering and Economics (CIFEr). New York, USA: IEEE; 2022. pp. 1-8. DOI: 10.1109/CIFEr52523.2022.9776208

[11] Sremac S, Tanackov I, Kopić M, Radović D. ANFIS model for determining the economic order quantity. Decision Making: Applications in Management and Engineering. 2018;**1**(2):81-92. DOI: 10.31181/dmame1802079s

[12] Hoang D, Wiegratz K. Machine learning methods in finance: Recent applications and prospects. European Financial Management. 2023;**29**:1657-1701. DOI: 10.1111/eufm.12408

[13] Bangun D, Efendi S, Sembiring R. Analysis of data classification accuracy using ANFIS algorithm modification with k-medoids clustering. Sinkron.

2022;**7**(3):2080-2088. DOI: 10.33395/sinkron.v7i3.11610

[14] Guillen A, Herrera L, Rubio G, Pomares H, Lendasse A, Rojas I. New method for instance or prototype selection using mutual information in time series prediction. Neurocomputing. 2010;**73**(10-12):2030-2038. DOI: 10.1016/j.neucom.2009.11.031

[15] Ansarullah SI, Mohsin Saif S, Abdul Basit Andrabi S, Kumhar SH, Kirmani MM, Kumar DP. An intelligent and reliable hyperparameter optimization machine learning model for early heart disease assessment using imperative risk attributes. Journal of Healthcare Engineering. 2022;**2022**. DOI: 10.1109/CIFEr52523.2022.9776208

[16] Shah MI, Javed MF, Alqahtani A, Aldrees A. Environmental assessment based surface water quality prediction using hyper-parameter optimized machine learning models based on consistent big data. Process Safety and Environmental Protection. 2021;**151**:324-340. DOI: 10.1016/j.psep.2021.05.026

[17] Ghashami F, Kamyar K. Performance evaluation of ANFIS and GA-ANFIS for predicting stock market indices. International Journal of Economics and Finance. 2021;**13**(7):1-1. DOI: 10.5539/ijef.v13n7p1

[18] Rahbar MA. Evaluation of the hybrid method of genetic algorithm and adaptive neural-fuzzy network (ANFIS) model in predicting the bankruptcy of companies listed on the Tehran stock exchange. Journal of Applied Research on Industrial Engineering. 2022;**9**(3):274-290. DOI: 10.22105/jarie.2021.254142.1204